ROBERT HENRYSON

ROBERT HENRYSON

A Study of the
Major Narrative Poems

JOHN MacQUEEN

AT THE CLARENDON PRESS
1967

Oxford University Press, Ely House, London W. 1

GLASGOW NEW YORK TORONTO MELBOURNE WELLINGTON
CAPE TOWN SALISBURY IBADAN NAIROBI LUSAKA ADDIS ABABA
BOMBAY CALCUTTA MADRAS KARACHI LAHORE DACCA
KUALA LUMPUR HONG KONG TOKYO

PRINTED IN GREAT BRITAIN

1391835
PREFACE

I AM grateful to the friends who in various ways have helped to lessen the imperfections of this book—Dr. William Beattie, the late Professor John Butt, Dr. J. Durkan, Professor Denys Hay, Dr. I. A. Jamieson, Priscilla Jenkins, Professor James Kinsley, Robin Lorimer, Mgr. David McRoberts, Fr. Anthony Ross, Dr. Tom Scott, Mrs. Angela West, and the members of classes in the University of Edinburgh and elsewhere with whom I have at different times discussed Henryson's poetry. Miss E. M. Brown has compiled the index. My colleague, Dr. R. G. Nicholson, has made a number of valuable observations, which I have been able to incorporate in my text; one, the correctness of which seems self-evident, but which I have not been able to incorporate, is that the phrase 'slew baith tame and wyld' (*The Lion and the Mouse*, 192) refers to confiscations of land and executions which affected Lowlanders and Highlanders alike during the reign of James III. I am particularly indebted to Miss Brown and Dr. Nicholson. H. Harvey Wood and Messrs. Oliver and Boyd have graciously given me permission to quote from their edition of Henryson. The Clarendon Press reader has saved me from many inaccuracies and infelicities. I am sure that Henryson himself, despite his celebrated sympathy for mice, would have concurred with me in finding these verses by Ariston an appropriate conclusion:

Ὦ μύες, εἰ μὲν ἐπ' ἄρτον ἐληλύθατ' ἐς μυχὸν ἄλλον
στείχετ' (ἐπεὶ λιτὴν οἰκέομεν καλύβην)
Οὗ καὶ πίονα τυρὸν ἀποδρέψεσθε καὶ αὔην
ἰσχάδα καὶ δεῖπνον συχνὸν ἀπὸ σκυβάλων·
Εἰ δ' ἐν ἐμαῖς βίβλοισι πάλιν καταθήξετ' ὀδόντα,
κλαύσεσθ' οὐκ ἀγαθὸν κῶμον ἐπερχόμενοι.

CONTENTS

I

INTRODUCTION: HENRYSON'S *MILIEU*

Thence arts o'er all the northern world advance.
POPE, *Essay on Criticism*, 711

THE precise dates of Robert Henryson's birth and death remain unknown, but both probably belong to the fifteenth century, a period about which there are still many misconceptions.[1] Past accounts of fifteenth-century Scottish history have usually emphasized the near anarchy of the country. For this there is some justification. All the kings who came to the throne during the century did so as minors. When James I succeeded his father in 1406 he was eleven and had just begun his eighteen years of captivity in England. He returned in 1424, and in 1437 was murdered at Perth. James II was crowned at six, and for much of his reign Livingstons, Crichtons, and Douglases fought to obtain control of his person and the kingdom. In 1460 he was killed at Roxburgh by the explosion of one of his own cannons. James III was nine years old when he succeeded. His reign was notorious for the 'Bell-the-Cat' episode, the murder of Robert Cochrane and others at Lauder Bridge, and in 1488 he was himself murdered after his

[1] The best general account of Scottish history during the period is W. Croft Dickinson, *Scotland from the Earliest Times to 1603* (Edinburgh, 1961). Particular studies of major importance are E. W. M. Balfour-Melville, *James I, King of Scots* (London, 1936); A. I. Dunlop, *The Life and Times of James Kennedy, Bishop of St. Andrews* (Edinburgh, 1950); R. L. Mackie, *King James IV of Scotland* (Edinburgh, 1958).

defeat by rebels at Sauchieburn near Stirling. His fifteen-year-
old son who succeeded as James IV was on the side of the
rebels. Other notable incidents of the period are the battle
of Harlaw (1411), the murder of the earl of Douglas by James
II in 1452, the forcible suppression of the Black Douglases in
1455, and the conspiracies of the duke of Albany against his
brother James III between 1479 and 1485.

The violence of the times is undeniable. But it is easy,
especially perhaps for the twentieth-century student, to
overemphasize violence in a late medieval and early Renaissance context. During the fifteenth century prosperity increased almost without reference to external turbulence. One
might, for instance, compare with the hostile account of a
primitive and poverty-stricken Scotland written in 1435 by
the Italian diplomat and humanist Aeneas Sylvius (later
Pope Pius II) the much more favourable report given to the
king of Spain in 1498 by his ambassador, Pedro de Ayala.[1]
Even when one allows for bias and exaggeration on the part
of both writers, the change of circumstance is self-evident.
There is much evidence too for the growing importance of
the new Third Estate, the merchants of the burghs—an
estate which on at least one occasion became the object of
Robert Henryson's satire. Indeed, his fable, *The Two Mice*,
which describes both the comfort of the burgesses and the
sudden violence with which it was liable to be interrupted,
might almost serve as the type of Scottish burgh life in the
fifteenth century.

[1] See W. Croft Dickinson, Gordon Donaldson, and Isabel A. Milne,
A Source Book of Scottish History (London and Edinburgh, 1963), II. 2–6.
Contrast, for instance, the description of houses in the two accounts.

Thy mangerie is mingit all with cair,
Thy guse is gude, thy gansell sour as gall.
The subcharge of thy service is bot sair,
Sa sall thou find heir efterwart na ffall.
(183–6)

One must emphasize, it should be noted, the 'mangerie',
the 'guse', and the 'subcharge' equally with the 'cair'.

The prosperity was not limited to material comfort. Much
of it found expression in church-building—in particular, the
collegiate establishments for secular priests so characteristic
of fifteenth-century Scottish architecture. Especially notable
are the College of Lincluden near Dumfries (*c.* 1400), that of
Seton in East Lothian (*c.* 1470), and the chapel of Roslin near
Edinburgh (*c.* 1450). Edinburgh or its neighbourhood had
four collegiate churches, St. Giles, Trinity, Restalrig, and
Corstorphine. This too was the period during which Tor-
phichen Priory was built and Melrose and Paisley Abbeys
were reconstructed. Continental influence is illustrated by
the fact that one at least of the architects at Melrose was of
French birth, and even more by the style at Roslin. Secular
architecture flourished. The fifteenth century saw the development of the full possibilities of the characteristically Scottish
Tower House. Renaissance influence began to appear in the
greater buildings—for instance the fifteenth-century range
beside the west curtain of Caerlaverock Castle in Dumfries-
shire, much of Linlithgow Palace, and in particular the Great
Hall of Stirling Castle. This last was probably the work of
Robert Cochrane, chief among James III's favourites who were
hanged at Lauder Bridge. Cochrane's stature as an architect
has not yet been fully recognized.

Since Henryson is believed to have been a schoolmaster, it is especially important to notice the developments in education during this period. In England, as A. F. Leach remarked,[1] 'so far as education is concerned, the fifteenth century was not one of decadence but of progress. A great development of educational foundations took place, alike in the re-endowment and enlargement of old schools and the erection of new schools and colleges.' After the failure or suppression of the universities of Northampton (1238–65), Salisbury (1238–c. 1325), and Stamford (1333)[2], no new universities appeared. But during the fifteenth century many colleges were founded at the existing universities; at Cambridge, King's (1441), Queens' (1448 and 1465), St. Catherine's (1473), and Jesus (1496); at Oxford, Lincoln (1427), All Souls (1438), and Magdalen (1458). Typical grammar schools of the period are Eton (1440), Magdalen College School, Oxford (1448), and Tong in Staffordshire (1410).

Of the many continental universities founded during the fifteenth century, one may single out Leipzig (1409), Louvain (1426), Basle (1460), Tübingen (1477), Uppsala (1477), and Copenhagen (1479). New types of school, too, were beginning to appear. In the Netherlands and Germany the Brethren of the Common Life[3] (founded by Geert de Groote, who died in 1384) laid great stress on teaching, 'founding schools all over the Netherlands, and later in Germany, where a general

[1] A. F. Leach, *The Schools of Medieval England* (2nd edit., London, 1916), p. 235.

[2] See especially Leach, op. cit., pp. 158, 165.

[3] See A. Hyma, *The Christian Renaissance* (New York, 1925). I have only been able to consult Chapters 1–3, published as *The 'Devotio Moderna' or Christian Renaissance* (Grand Rapids, n.d.). Particularly relevant are pp. 91–98, 122–35.

education was offered, unsurpassed in quality and without fees'.[1] Thomas à Kempis (*c.* 1380–1471)[2] was associated with the brethren, as was the great schoolmaster Alexander Hegius (1433–98). The early German humanist, Rudolph Agricola (1443–85) studied in their schools, as did Nicholas of Cusa (*c.* 1400–64) and Erasmus.

In Italy *La casa Giocosa*, the more famous of the new humanist boarding-schools, was set up in 1423 at Mantua by Vittorino da Feltre (1378–1446). Superficially, the distinguishing feature of these schools was the study of Augustan Latin with a little classical Greek, the cultivation of rhetoric at the expense of scholastic logic, and care for the physical as well as the mental and moral well-being of the pupil. The 'barbarism' and vitality of medieval Latin was carefully excluded. But these features are not the most important. Woodward's summary[3] is more perceptive: 'The general aims of the Mantuan school, as they were developed during the two and twenty years in which Vittorino stamped upon it the impress of his remarkable personality, was [*sic*] to effect a reconciliation of the moral and religious teaching of the church with classical instruction on lines approved by Quintilian and the knightly disciplines of the Italian Castello, all being suffused with something of the Greek feeling for grace and harmony. . . . His education moreover was held by him to be a thoroughly

---

[1] *Oxford Dictionary of the Christian Church* (London, 1957), s.v. 'Brethren of the Common Life'.

[2] The *De Imitatione Christi* was translated into English *c.* 1450. See H. S. Bennett, *Chaucer and the Fifteenth Century* (Oxford, 1947), p. 306.

[3] W. H. Woodward, *Studies in Education during the Age of the Renaissance, 1400–1600* (Cambridge, 1924), p. 12. Cf. also his *Vittorino da Feltre and other Humanist Educators* (Cambridge, 1897); G. Biasuz (ed.), *Vita di Vittorino da Feltre* (Padova, 1948).

practical discipline, preparing youth for a life of action, and
training both mind and character for the due exercise of judgement in affairs. His was a school for statesmen, for adminis-
trators, for high ecclesiastics, for captains of distinction, for
schoolmasters like-minded with himself.' The doctrine of
the movement may be found in the *De Ingenuis Moribus*
(*c.* 1392) of P. P. Vergerius, the *De Studiis et Literis* (*c.* 1405)
of Lionardo Bruni d'Arezzo, the *De Liberorum Educatione*
(1449) of Aeneas Sylvius, and the *De Ordine Docendi et
Studendi* (1459) of Battista Guarino.[1]

On at least one level, fifteenth-century foundations of three
universities, St. Andrews (1411), Glasgow (1451), and
Aberdeen (1495), links Scotland directly with English, and
more particularly European, educational movements. So too
with colleges. At St. Andrews Bishop Kennedy founded in
1450 St. Salvator's College, perhaps on the model of New
College, Oxford, but with an eye on contemporary reforms
in the University of Paris.[2] Bologna, Paris, and Cologne are
mentioned in the foundation documents of Glasgow University, but St. Andrews and Louvain also contributed.[3] The
European connexions of the universities are easy to demonstrate. Laurence of Lindores (*c.* 1375–1437), first Master of
St. John's College in St. Andrews University, had taught in
Paris; his writings on physics and psychology held the field
in German universities for at least fifty years.[4] Bishop Kennedy

[1] Translations may be found in Woodward, *Studies.*

[2] R. G. Cant, *The University of St. Andrews: A Short History* (Edinburgh,
1946), p. 25; A. I. Dunlop, op. cit., pp. 282–5.

[3] J. Durkan, *William Turnbull* (Glasgow, 1951), pp. 34–45; C. Innes (ed.),
Munimenta Alme Universitatis Glasguensis (Glasgow, 1854), II. 20 ff.

[4] J. H. Baxter, 'Four "New" Medieval Scottish Authors', *S.H.R.* xxv
(1928), pp. 92 ff.

was a St. Andrews Master of Arts and a Louvain Bachelor of Canon Law. He travelled widely. Dr. Dunlop says[1] of him: 'The Bishop of St. Andrews was at home in the courts of Popes, princes and potentates in Italy, France and the Burgundian dominions; he had experienced the wealth and power of the great Italian and Flemish cities; and in his youth he had seen the devastated fields and starving peasantry of unredeemed France.' His contemporary, Bishop Turnbull, the founder of Glasgow University, was as cosmopolitan. He was a St. Andrews Master of Arts, a Louvain Bachelor of Canon Law, and a Pavia Doctor of Canon Law. He arrived at Louvain in 1431 and was in Italy from 1433 to 1439, and again before his death. Dr. Durkan has emphasized[2] the intellectual brilliance of the circle which surrounded him at Pavia— Lorenzo Valla, Maffeo Vegio, Francesco Filelfo, Theodore of Gaza. At the same time Poggio was a secretary in the Roman Curia. Of Bishop Turnbull's colleagues in the foundation of Glasgow, Andrew of Durisdeer was a graduate of St. Andrews and Paris, David Cadzow, the first Rector, was a licentiate of canon law, perhaps of Bologna; Duncan Bunch, vice-chancellor in 1454, was a graduate of Cologne. Pope Nicholas V, whom Turnbull probably knew personally and who issued the bull establishing Glasgow University, was a lover of arts and sciences who founded the Vatican Library. 'He was the first, and probably the best, of the Renaissance Popes, of blameless personal life, free from nepotism and anxious to reconcile religion with the new learning.'[3]

The history of the medieval Scottish grammar school has

[1] Dunlop, op. cit., p. 424.   [2] Durkan, op. cit., pp. 15 ff.
[3] *Oxford Dictionary of the Christian Church*, s.v. 'Nicholas V'.

yet to be written, and the following account is necessarily tentative. For the earliest stages more evidence is provided by Irish than by Scottish records. The schools attached to Irish and Scottish monasteries of Celtic type were probably originally directed by the 'scribe', the Master of the Scriptorium.[1] After the early tenth century, however, his place seems to have been taken by the 'man of learning', the *fer-léginn* or Master of the Schools. The *Vita* of the Welsh St. Cadog, written by Lifris about 1100, describes how Cadog went to an Irish monastic school, that of Mochutu at Lismore.[2] St. Cadog probably belongs to the sixth century, but when Lifris states that in Ireland he studied the seven liberal arts, he may to some extent be assuming that at an earlier date the curriculum resembled that offered by a *fer-léginn* of his own time. Whether or not this is so, the instruction probably followed the contemporary European pattern of the *trivium*, grammar, dialectic, and rhetoric, followed by the *quadrivium*, arithmetic, geometry, music, and astronomy. The likelihood of this is increased by a decision of the Irish Synod of Clane in 1162, which stated that only pupils of Armagh were to obtain the position of *fer-léginn* in a school attached to any church in Ireland. MacNeill[3] rightly pointed out that the decree was equivalent to a recognition of the school of Armagh as a national university with power to issue the

[1] K. Hughes, 'The Distribution of Irish Scriptoria and Centres of Learning' in N. K. Chadwick (ed.), *Studies in the Early British Church* (Cambridge, 1958), p. 248.

[2] A. W. Wade-Evans, *Vitae Sanctorum Britanniae et Genealogiae* (Cardiff, 1944), p. 48.

[3] E. MacNeill, *Phases of Irish History* (Dublin, 1919), pp. 284–5. The *Catholic Encyclopaedia*, s.v. 'Universities' refers to a University at Dublin in 1320 and one at Drogheda in 1465.

licence *ubique docendi*. In an almost exactly similar manner the cathedral school of Paris developed into the University of Paris. One might compare too the later English and Scottish requirement that the principal master of a grammar school should be an M.A.[1] In Britain, one result of the requirement was a certain lowering of the status of the grammar school, which more and more became concerned with the *trivium*, while the *quadrivium*, together with philosophy, occupied the university candidate for the degree of Master of Arts. The decree may indicate the beginning of a similar process in Ireland.

The effect of Armagh on Scotland may be indicated by the fact[2] that in 1169, the year, ironically, in which began the Norman invasion which eventually brought the University of Armagh to a premature end, the king of Ireland, Ruaidhrí O'Conchubhair, established and endowed a new professorship there for the benefit of students from Ireland and Scotland. Under the year 1164, Dubsidi, *fer-léginn* of Iona, is mentioned in the *Annals of Ulster*.[3] The latinized form of the word is *ferlanus*, which at St. Andrews was a term still in use during the early years of the thirteenth century.[4] The Culdees, the early monastic community of St. Andrews, had earlier been transformed into the collegiate church of St. Mary of the Rock,

---

[1] In *Extracts from the Council Register of the Burgh of Aberdeen 1398–1570* (Spalding Club, 1844), pp. 4–5, one of the requirements for the *Magister Scolarum* is that he should have graduated in arts.

[2] MacNeill, loc. cit.

[3] W. F. Skene, *Chronicles of the Picts and Scots* (Edinburgh, 1867), p. 372. The complete text of A.U. was edited by W. M. Hennessey and B. Macarthy (Dublin, 1887–1901).

[4] *Liber Cartarum Prioratus Sancti Andree* (Bannatyne Club, 1841), pp. 316–18.

and as such claimed some share in episcopal elections until
the middle of the thirteenth century. The existence of a
Culdee community may explain the survival of the term. It
is probably safe to assume that elsewhere, wherever a major
Culdee community had existed, a *fer-léginn* and school giving
instructions in the *trivium* were also to be found. Abernethy,
for instance, was a major Culdee establishment, and about
1100[1] Berbeadh was *rector scolarum de Abyrnethyn*, 'schoolmaster of Abernethy'.

English and European institutions were introduced by
Queen Margaret and her sons, especially David I. Margaret
superseded the Culdee establishment at Dunfermline with a
Benedictine monastery. Under Alexander I Scone became
a priory of Augustinian canons. David established communities of Augustinian canons which gradually displaced or
absorbed the Culdees of St. Andrews, St. Serfs, Monymusk,
and Abernethy. Dunblane, Dunkeld, Brechin, Rosemarkie,
and Lismore eventually became the cathedrals of diocesan
bishops. In all cases, however, it is probable that the school
survived and became an integral part of the new system.
Schools were also sometimes attached to the new monastic
foundations of continental pattern, and to friaries and the
newer collegiate establishments. The schoolmasters of
cathedral schools were under the authority of the chancellor
of the cathedral; those of abbey schools were appointed by
the abbot, and those of collegiate schools by the provost. It
should be added that by the fifteenth century the majority of
the parish churches had been granted to cathedrals, monasteries, and collegiate churches, and that dependent grammar

[1] *Liber Cartartum Prioratus Sancti Andree*, p. 116.

schools were often many miles from the mother establishment.

Grant[1] mentions the following grammar schools as already in existence before 1400. The dates indicate not foundation but merely the first occasion on which the school or schoolmaster is mentioned in records which happen to have survived:

Eleventh century: Abernethy (1100).

Twelfth century: St. Andrews (1120), Roxburgh (1128), Perth, Stirling (1160), Lanark (1163), Linlithgow (1187).

Thirteenth century: Ayr (1233), Aberdeen (1256), Glasgow (1258), Kelso (1260).

Fourteenth century: Montrose (1329), Cupar (1357), Haddington (1383), Tranent (1392).

The grammar school of Edinburgh (*scolas gramaticales ecclesie de Edimburgh*) appears in 1378 in the Cartulary of the University of Montpellier.[2]

Grammar and logic are indicated as the main subjects of the school curriculum by the *Statuta Ecclesie Aberdonensis* (1256)[3] which state: 'Dignitas autem cancellarii est quod ipse providebit de ydoneo magistro qui habeat regimen scolarum de Aberden qui sciat pueros tam in grammatica

---

[1] J. Grant, *History of the Burgh and Parish Schools of Scotland* (London and Glasgow, 1876), pp. 1–75. A list of sixty-four Scottish pre-Reformation schools compiled by Dr. Durkan will be found in D. McRoberts (ed.), *Essays on the Scottish Reformation* (Glasgow, 1962), p. 168.

[2] J. H. Baxter, *Copiale Prioratus Sanctiandree* (London, 1930), p. xxxvii, note 1.

[3] *Registrum Episcopatus Aberdonensis* (Spalding Club, 1845), II. 45. For the ideals of medieval education, cf. particularly Vincent of Beauvais, *De Eruditione Filiorum Nobilium*, ed. A. Steiner (Cambridge, Mass., 1938).

quam in logica erudire.' But details of curriculum are best indicated by continental sources. In the twelfth century the German Conrad of Hirsau mentions[1] twenty-one authors who figured in the grammar curriculum. Conrad may have listed them in the order in which they were studied; they are Donatus, Cato (the Moral Distiches), Aesop, Avianus, Sedulius, Juvencus, Prosper of Aquitaine, Theodulus, Arator, Prudentius, Cicero (*De Amicitia*, *De Senectute*), Sallust, Boethius, Lucan, Horace (*Ars Poetica*), Ovid (*Fasti* and *Ex Ponto*), Juvenal, 'Homerus' (the *Ilias Latina*), Persius, Statius, and Virgil. The school study of rhetoric may also be illustrated by the twelfth and thirteenth-century *Arts of Poetry*, notably those by Geoffrey of Vinsauf and John of Garland. The logic curriculum probably consisted essentially of the 'old' Aristotelian logic and the commentaries of Boethius. Scottish schools may have had fewer books than French or German, but their probable resources should not be under-estimated.

How far continental influence reached fifteenth-century Scottish grammar schools must meanwhile remain something of a mystery. But when the principal master was customarily an M.A., and many Scottish students attended continental universities—at a time too when the Scottish universities were themselves particularly open to continental influence— it seems reasonable to assume some transference of ideas and practices. The close trading links between Scotland and the Low Countries should not be forgotten. Another probable source of influence is the Council of Basle (1431–49) which

[1] Cf. E. R. Curtius, *European Literature and the Latin Middle Ages*, translated by W. R. Trask (London, 1953), p. 49.

many Scottish clerics attended.[1] Leach notes[2] that Duke
Humphrey of Gloucester used the council as a means of get-
ting from Italian scholars translations into Latin of the Greek
philosophers and the Greek fathers, and of Boccaccio into
French. So too during the fifteenth century it became important that senior civil servants and diplomatists should have
mastered the humanist Latin style of the Papal Curia.[3] Here,
one important piece of evidence is the *Oratio Scotorum ad
Regem Ricardum Tertium*, delivered to Richard III at Notting-
ham in 1484 by Archibald Whitelaw, James III's secretary of
state and former tutor.[4] Whitelaw was born about 1420,
determined at St. Andrews in 1437, and became Licentiate in
1439. He is found teaching at Cologne in the 1440s, and in
1454 he was on the St. Andrews faculty.[5] He had become
James's tutor by 1459, and in 1465 describes himself as
secretary and schoolmaster to the king. He had considerable
diplomatic experience, and held the post of secretary until his
retirement in 1493. Ecclesiastically he was archdeacon of
Lothian and subdean of Glasgow. He died in 1498. The Latinity of his *Oratio* is that of a Christian humanist, modelled on
Cicero, to whom in the course of eight pages he refers four
times, notably in the sentence. 'In te enim sunt rei militaris
pericia, virtus, felicitas et auctoritas, quae omnia in optimo
exercitus principe Cicero de Pompei laudibus requirenda
commemorat'.[6] The reference is to Cicero's *De Imperio Cn.*

[1] J. H. Burns, *Scottish Churchmen and the Council of Basle* (Glasgow, 1962).
[2] Op. cit., p. 251. Cf. R. Weiss, *Humanism in England during the Fifteenth Century* (2nd edit., Oxford, 1957), pp. 50–52.
[3] Weiss, op. cit., p. 181.
[4] *Bannatyne Miscellany*, II (Edinburgh, 1836), pp. 41–48. See the brief notices in Durkan, *Turnbull*, pp. 42–43, 56–57.
[5] Dunlop, op. cit., p. 289 n.   [6] pp. 42–43.

Pompei, the oration which to some extent formed the model for Whitelaw's, and in particular to x. 28, 'Ego enim sic existimo, in summo imperatore quattuor has res inesse oportere: scientiam rei militaris, virtutem, auctoritatem, felicitatem.' In addition, Whitelaw quotes Statius three times, Virgil five times; Seneca, Sallust, and Livy once each. On one occasion[1] he gives the etymology of a Greek word which he uses (*amnestia, verbo Graeco, id est, iniuriarum oblivione*). Whitelaw's humanism is also indicated by those of his books which have survived;[2] a Lucan, printed at Louvain *c.* 1475: a Horace, printed at Venice in 1478 and glossed by Whitelaw in his own hand: an Appian, printed at Venice in 1477: a Sallust, printed at Venice in 1481: the commentary on the orations of Cicero by Asconius, discovered at St. Gall by the Italian humanist Poggio in 1414 and printed at Venice in 1477, and finally, rather unexpectedly,[3] the *De Animalibus* of Albertus Magnus, printed at Mantua in 1479. The number of Italian books is significant. Whitelaw also owned an Italian[4] manuscript (Aberdeen University MS. 214), containing Florus, Orosius, and the *Historia de Origine Troianorum* of Dares Phrygius. His life and work seem to belong to the tradition of *La casa Giocosa*, and it should be noted that he is an exact contemporary of Henryson.

Almost certainly Whitelaw did not acquire his mature Latin style at a Scottish grammar school; he lived at too early

[1] p. 47.

[2] J. Durkan and A. Ross, *Early Scottish Libraries* (Glasgow, 1961), p. 159.

[3] Dr. Durkan (*Turnbull*, p. 43) has suggested reasons for the presence of the Albertus.

[4] So Durkan, *Turnbull*, p. 56. M. R. James, *Catalogue of the Medieval Manuscripts in the University Library Aberdeen* (Cambridge, 1932), p. 59, thinks French.

a date. But it should be noted that as tutor to the young James III he was himself a schoolmaster whose position bore some resemblance to that of Vittorino da Feltre at the court of the marquis of Mantua. His oration may prove no more than that by the end of the reign of James III one Scot had acquired something of the ideals of the Italian humanist schoolmasters. But it remains possible, and even probable, that other contemporary Scottish schoolmasters were following similar paths.

Inevitably fifteenth-century Scottish vernacular literature was affected by the new movement.[1] James I's *Kingis Quair* already shows some stirrings of interest.[2] The poem is saturated with Chaucerian reminiscences, but to a greater extent than any of Chaucer's poems it is a discussion and apparent solution of a philosophic problem—the relation of Fortune to the individual. James began not from Chaucer but from Boethius. It should be remembered that James had been a prisoner at the court of Henry V of England, himself a patron of scholarship, whose brother Humphrey of Gloucester was a munificent friend to the new learning. Aeneas Sylvius, at the time of his mission to James's court, was regarded as a scholar and humanist rather than a churchman.

At a first glance there is little to connect Henryson with the intellectual milieu which has just been described. But the

[1] It is an extraordinary fact that neither H. S. Bennett nor the late C. S. Lewis, both of whom consider Scottish literature at some length, includes any reference to the foundation documents of the Scottish universities in the bibliographies to their volumes of the *Oxford History of English Literature* (Bennett, *Chaucer and the Fifteenth Century*; Lewis, *English Literature in the Sixteenth Century*, Oxford, 1954).

[2] J. MacQueen, 'Tradition and the Interpretation of the *Kingis Quair*', *R.E.S.*, N.S. XII (1961), pp. 117 ff.

evidence is more suggestive than has generally been realized.[1]
On the title-page of Bassandyne's edition of the *Morall
Fabillis* (1571) and elsewhere, Henryson is described as schoolmaster of Dunfermline. Sir Francis Kinaston,[2] writing in the
seventeenth century on the authority of 'Sr. Tho: Eriskin
late earle of Kelly & divers aged schollers of the Scottish
nation', calls him chief schoolmaster in Dunfermline. 'Schoolmaster' in fact normally implies 'chief schoolmaster'. In the
Lament for the Makaris, printed in 1508, Dunbar mentions
Henryson's death, and again connects him with Dunfermline:

> In Dunfermelyne he (Death) hes done roune
> With Maister Robert Henrisoun.

In the first place, then, a connexion of the poet with Dunfermline may be regarded as certain, a connexion which in
the fifteenth century had connotations rather different from
those of the present day. The town was then one of the most
important centres in Scotland. It had grown up around the
royal palace and the Benedictine abbey, Holy Trinity, Dunfermline, a daughter house of Christ Church, Canterbury,
founded *c.* 1074 by St. Margaret, wife of Malcolm Canmore.
The existing Norman church was begun in the reign of
David I, and probably completed by 1150. Dunfermline was
no rural backwater. Throughout its history town and church
were closely associated with the Scottish royal family. Before
Henryson's time the monastic guest-house had become the
royal palace in which James I was born. The more lurid side

[1] M. Y. Stearns, e.g., in his *Robert Henryson* (New York, 1949), pp. 8 ff.,
is aware of many of the facts, but does not set them in a proper context.

[2] Quoted, e.g., in H. Harvey Wood, *Poems and Fables of Robert Henryson*
(2nd edit., Edinburgh, 1958), p. xii. (All quotations from *Orpheus and
Eurydice* and the *Testament of Cresseid* are based on this edition.)

of palace life may be gathered from Dunbar's poem, 'The Wowing of the King at Dunfermline'. The church was almost a Scottish Westminster Abbey; it was the burial place of eight kings, four queens, five princes, and two princesses, among them St. Margaret, David I, and Robert the Bruce. Quite apart from the importance of Dunfermline itself, Fife was almost the centre of the Scottish kingdom, containing as it did the bishopric, later archbishopric, the Augustinian priory, and the University of St. Andrews, Falkland Palace, the monastic houses of Balmerino, Lindores, Culross, St. Serf's, and Inchcolm, besides many important fishing and trading burghs along the coast of the Firth of Forth and the North Sea.

The grammar school of Dunfermline with which Henryson is probably to be connected was thus a place of some importance. Probably it was one of the most ancient in Scotland. No early references have survived, but the abbey was preceded by a Culdee foundation, and it is not likely that when in 1160 the grammar schools of Perth and Stirling were subject to Dunfermline,[1] Dunfermline itself lacked a school. The master's status corresponded to that of his school. References to Henryson as schoolmaster are late, but the title *Maister* usually given to him is almost certainly an indication that he was an M.A., and therefore properly qualified for the position of schoolmaster. He does not appear as a graduate of Glasgow or St. Andrews:[2] the probable inference is that he studied at a continental university. Under fifteenth-century conditions, Oxford or Cambridge is less likely.

[1] Grant, op. cit., pp. 4–5.
[2] C. Innes, op. cit.: J. Maitland Anderson, *Early Records of the University of St. Andrews* (Edinburgh, 1926).

A Master of Arts was skilled in the *trivium*, grammar, rhetoric, logic, and in the *quadrivium*, geometry, arithmetic, music, and astronomy. He was also thoroughly acquainted with the old and new Aristotle.[1] Henryson's works contain several indications that he was a graduate in arts and a schoolmaster. First, the *trivium*. As has already been indicated, Aesop was a standard grammar-school text, and Henryson's treatment of the *Fabillis* is fully in accordance with the educational theories of the chief medieval authority, Vincent of Beauvais,[2] and the later schoolmasters of the Renaissance. His comments are very much aimed at 'training both mind and character for the due exercise of judgement in affairs'.[3] Boethius' *De Consolatione* was also a *trivium* text, which Henryson used, together with the standard commentary of the Dominican Nicholas Trevet, as the basis for his *Orpheus and Eurydice*. Important too was the *De Genealogia Deorum* (*c.* 1360) of Boccaccio from which Henryson derived material for each of his three major poems. The *Genealogia* may not have included much that was positively new, but it was highly regarded by the Italian schoolmasters; thus in 1434 Vittorino wrote 'that if any one possessed a copy of the book called 'De Genealogia Deorum' and were prepared to part with it, he should at once offer it to Master Vittorino who will purchase it and will further regard such offer as a great personal favour'.[4] That Henryson knew the school rhetorical treatises is shown by his skilful variations of stylistic level,

[1] See A. O. Norton, *Readings in the History of Education. Mediaeval Universities* (Cambridge, Mass., 1909), pp. 135–40. Cf. also J. H. Baxter, op. cit., p. 456.

[2] See above, p. 11, n. 3.   [3] Woodward, *Studies*, p. 12.

[4] Woodward, *Vittorino*, p. 69.

and by such formal descriptive passages as the series of planet portraits in the *Testament of Cresseid*. Henryson too was skilled in logic—in particular he tends, most notably in the fable of *The Wolf and the Lamb*, to use the syllogism as a logical basis for the construction of a stanza.

Henryson's knowledge of Aristotle and the *quadrivium* is shown by his use of the *De Anima*, *Parva Naturalia* and *Metaphysics*, Boethius' *De Musica* and *De Arithmetica*, and astronomical writings like the *De Sphaera* of Sacrobosco.

Other Latin writings to influence him were the *De Trinitate* of St. Augustine, the works of Fulgentius, the *De Sacramentis* of Hugh of St. Victor, and the *Summa Theologica* of Thomas Aquinas. His writings abound in echoes and adaptations of the Vulgate, sometimes in a form which indicates that he was familiar with earlier allegorical commentaries on the Biblical text.

Nor was Henryson's knowledge and appreciation confined to Latin literature. We have evidence that he was acquainted with the *Kingis Quair*, with popular Scottish alliterative poems, with much of Chaucer and Lydgate, and with a number of works in French. He seems to have had access to books printed by Caxton in the 1480s. Nothing directly suggests that he knew Greek, but the *Orpheus and Eurydice* is proof enough that he was aware of the importance of Greek studies.[1]

This is not all. The *Testament* shows Henryson's considerable medical knowledge. The *Fabillis*, particularly *The Sheep and the Dog*, *The Wolf and the Lamb*, and *The Fox, the Wolf and the Husbandman*, show a command of legal language and procedure which Henryson can scarcely have gained casually.

[1] The evidence for these statements is set out in subsequent chapters.

Long ago Laing[1] suggested that the poet was to be identified
with the 'Magister Robertus Henrisone in artibus licenciatus
et in decretis bachalarius' who on 10 September 1462 was
incorporated in Glasgow University, probably to give
lectures in law.[2] The title *Magister* and the licentiate in arts,
which in fifteenth-century Scottish universities was essentially
identical with the M.A.,[3] go far to prove the identity of this
Robert Henryson with the poet: the poet's legal knowledge is
certainly consonant with the possession of a bachelorship in
decreets. In the Prologue to *The Lion and the Mouse* Henryson
makes Aesop claim to have studied canon and civil law in the
schools of Rome. This is quite outside the usual tradition of
the life of Aesop. But Rome had schools of canon and civil
law for poor foreign students throughout the fourteenth and
fifteenth centuries.[4] The convention of the dream-vision used
in the Prologue allowed a poet to project aspects of his own
character on to the persons of his dream. As it is in any case
remarkable to find so precise a reference to papal institutions
in a secular Scottish work of the time, it seems reasonable to
assume that Henryson is here drawing on his own knowledge; perhaps even that he had himself studied canon and
civil law in the schools of Rome. A good deal of evidence
certainly suggests that he was the *venerabilis vir* incorporated
in Glasgow University.

One should perhaps add that Glasgow University may have
been intended primarily as a school of legal studies modelled

---

[1] D. Laing, *Poems and Fables of Robert Henryson* (Edinburgh, 1865).

[2] C. Innes, op. cit. II. 69. Cf. J. D. Mackie, *The University of Glasgow,
1451–1951* (Glasgow, 1954), p. 53.

[3] R. G. Cant, op. cit., pp. 10, 18–19.

[4] *Encyclopedia Britannica*, s.v. 'Universities'.

on Bologna.[1] If this is so, it would not be surprising to find a Scot with Italian legal training incorporated in the recently founded *studium generale*.

Various factors may help to explain Henryson's transference from Glasgow to Dunfermline. In the first place, close connexions had existed between Bishop Turnbull, founder of Glasgow University, and Richard Bothwell, abbot of Dunfermline.[2] Thus the Turnbull arms appear in the new work carried out by Bothwell at the abbey. In the second place, it is obvious from the *Fabillis* that Henryson's treatment of legal practitioners and practices is something less than sympathetic. He may have welcomed the opportunity of turning from law to the more humanistic pursuits of the *trivium*. Transference from university to grammar-school teaching was more usual in the fifteenth than in the twentieth century, and for Henryson the move to so distinguished a school as that of Dunfermline may have meant a decided increase in status and emoluments.

One further piece of evidence confirms the portrait of the poet which has gradually emerged. In sixteenth-century England humanist schoolmasters and educational theorists contributed largely to the growth of the vocabulary by the conscious importation of words which they believed were needed. Sir Thomas Elyot was a distinguished exponent of

[1] H. Rashdall, *The Universities of Europe in the Middle Ages* (rev. edition by F. M. Powicke and A. B. Emden, London, 1936), II. 313. But cf. J. D. Mackie, op. cit., p. 8.

[2] I owe this suggestion to Father Anthony Ross, O.P. Cf. Durkan, *Turnbull*, p. 28. Cf. also Dr. Durkan's observation 'By 1468 we hear that the abbot of Dunfermline had provided a house for the town schoolmaster and lands and rents worth eleven merks yearly maintaining poor scholars to be taught there gratuitously. The gift of the schoolhouse may have encouraged Henryson to stay.' (D. McRoberts, op. cit., p. 157).

the practice. It has not hitherto been noticed that many words of a decidedly humanistic appearance are first to be found in Henryson's work. I have not attempted to be exhaustive, but the present rough list will serve to illustrate the point. The words either occur in Henryson for the first time as recorded in the *Oxford English Dictionary* or the *Dictionary of the Older Scottish Tongue*, or they are used by Henryson within a few years of their first appearance elsewhere.

A *per se*, boreal, brutal, capacity, correspond, decrepit, degenerate, diminute, elegant, equivalent, exorbitant, extol, figural, generable, idol ('mental image'), intricate, invention (as a rhetorical term), irrational, participant, radicate, rusticate, sapor, spoliate, toxicate, type, vilipend.

Henryson must then be regarded as in some sense a humanist. But his humanism is not of the Italian type. He heralds the Northern Renaissance, whose continuity with the Middle Ages extended even into the late seventeenth and early eighteenth century—there was no decisive break with the past. The remarks of Professor Weiss[1] on early English humanism are equally applicable to Henryson and Scotland:

'English humanism in the fifteenth century was very different in its manifestations from contemporary Italian humanism. Whereas in Italy the cult of the antique had completely transformed cultural values, in England we find neo-classicism absorbed into the sphere of scholasticism and used for the furtherance of scholastic ends. Moreover, in Italy humanism had been considered as a new intellectual system displacing or revising all the conceptions of the Middle Ages; but in England humanism was conceived not as a new cultural manifestation

[1] Weiss, op. cit., p. 179.

or a refinement in taste, but rather as a means of improving some aspects of scholasticism.'

Much of Henryson is to be found in these words—in particular the Henryson who knew and used Hugh of St. Victor, Aquinas, and Nicholas Trevet. The greatest difference between English and Scottish humanism of the period is the fact that at so early a date Robert Henryson gave memorable poetic expression to material which in England remained inarticulate until the time of Spenser. In a real sense he is the first of the University Wits.

II

ORPHEUS AND EURYDICE

Sed haec ratio quemadmodum in mundo est ex volubi-
litate circulorum, ita et in microcosmo in tantum praeter
vocem valet, ut sine ipsius perfectione etiam homo
symphoniis carens non constet.

ISIDORE, *Etymologiae*, III. xxiii. 2

There's not the smallest orb which thou beholds't
But in his motion like an angel sings,
Still quiring to the young-eyes cherubins;
But, whilst this muddy vesture of decay
Doth grossly close it in, we cannot hear it.

SHAKESPEARE, *Merchant of Venice*, V. i. 60–65

IN Scotland as in England there was no real break in poetic
theory between medieval times and the Renaissance. Especially in matters of style, diction, and decorum, Chaucer's art
of poetry differs only incidentally from that of Spenser. In
the previous chapter I have tried to show that Henryson was
himself a man of the early Renaissance, but even if the idea is
rejected, there should be no difficulty in accepting that manuals
of Renaissance poetic theory and technique, written after
Henryson's death, should have some relevance to his poetry.
The most immediately useful is probably *Ane Schort Treatise,
Conteining some Reulis and Cautelis to be observit and eschewit
in Scottis Poesie*, included by James VI in *The Essayes of a*

Prentise, in the Divine Art of Poesie.[1] The charge has been made,[2] it is true, that James cut himself off deliberately from earlier poetry in English, but this is to go too far. There is direct evidence, for instance, that James knew and approved both Chaucer and Henryson; when in Chapter VIII he calls the seven-line Chaucerian stanza 'Troilus verse' and describes it as suitable for 'tragicall materis, complaintis, or testamentis', he must have intended a favourable reference to Chaucer's *Troilus and Criseyde* and Henryson's *Testament of Cresseid.* It is at least suggestive that when in Chapter VII he describes Invention as 'ane of the cheif vertewis in a Poete', he is using a term which Henryson seems to have been the the first to adapt to English literary use.[3] And his emphasis in Chapter III on the use of alliteration in verse suggests strongly that he was well aware of earlier Scottish verse, in which alliteration was more usual than in verse written in southern England.

It is possible, however, to say more than that for James 'Scottis Poesie' included the poetry of Henryson—some at any rate of the observations which he makes are directly related to his reading of earlier Scots poetry. In Chapter III his remarks on diction and stylistic level are developed from the universal medieval and Renaissance concept of the three styles—high, middle and low—but developed in a way which has peculiarly Scottish overtones. He deals first with diction. It is necessary to 'waill your wordis according to the purpose'; high words accordingly he reserves for 'ane heich and learnit

[1] Ed. J. Craigie, *The Poems of James VI of Scotland* (Scottish Text Society, 1955) I. 65–83.
[2] Ibid., p. xiii.
[3] See above, Chapter I, *ad. fin.*

purpose', but somewhat unusually he includes pithiness as one of the major attributes of high style. Examples, however, are readily to be found in the *Testament of Cresseid*[1] and some part of the *Orpheus and Eurydice*. James seems to distinguish two middle styles; the lower appropriate for love poetry, the higher for tragic poetry. More unusual is his emphasis on 'corruptit and uplandis wordis' for the treatment of 'land-wart effairis'—an emphasis not present in the English and French theorists of the sixteenth century, but unusually apt for anyone writing on Scots poetry, which for a century and a half had been making comic use of a rustic vocabulary, just as for other purposes it had developed an elaborate aureate style. James insists too that the ornaments of style should follow the dictates of decorum: in this he is merely following the general European approach, but it is worthy of note that the ornaments which in Chapter IV he particularly singles out are '*Comparisons*, *Epithetis*, and *Proverbis*', all of which Henryson uses in close conformity with the rules set out in the *Treatise*.

These concepts, it may be said, affect only the external form of poetry, and in fact it was with the external form that James chiefly concerned himself. Even so, to realize the major stylistic features of a poem is to go some way towards full understanding. For the rest, Henryson himself indicates very precisely his concept of the substance of poetry, a concept which may be seen most readily in the comparatively brief *Orpheus and Eurydice*, which reaches its greatest complexity in the *Testament of Cresseid*, and which governs the seemingly

[1] See especially 'Conciseness and the *Testament of Cresseid*', Chapter 6 of A. C. Spearing's *Criticism and Medieval Poetry* (London, 1964).

disparate material of the *Morall Fabillis of Esope the Phrygian*.
It is nevertheless surprising that even the *Orpheus and Eurydice*
has received so little in the way of perceptive formal criticism.
One writer, for instance, remarks:[1] '*Orpheus and Eurydice* is
one of the very few poems of the Middle Ages that tells a
classical tale for its own sake, with no allegorical trappings.'
As the main narrative of the poem is followed by an allegorical
Moralitas which in the Bannatyne MS. extends to 218 lines,
the assumption, one presumes, is that narrative and *Moralitas*
should be considered each in isolation, or at least that the
Moralitas bears no vital relationship to the narrative. Such
an assumption begs several questions, on the answers to which
will depend the method of interpreting all Henryson's narrative poetry. Three points must be made. In the first place
it has been suggested[2] that the *Moralitas* as it appears in
Bannatyne is not wholly Henryson's. The suggestion is un-
supported by evidence, but even if it were established, the
fact would still remain that Henryson subjoined some kind
of allegorical *Moralitas*, and therefore had some kind of
allegorical intention. Henryson's sources for the poem seem
to indicate the same conclusion. He names Boethius' *De
Consolatione Philosophiae* with the standard commentary of
Nicholas Trevet (?1258–1328), the English Dominican
theologian, biblicist, Hebraist, historian, and classicist, best
known for his Anglo-Norman *Chronicle*, used by Chaucer
and Gower, the importance of whom for the history of learning has recently been emphasized by Miss Beryl Smalley in

[1] K. Wittig, *The Scottish Tradition in Literature* (Edinburgh and London,
1958), p. 44.
[2] H. Harvey Wood, op. cit., p. xxvii.

her *English Friars and Antiquity in the Early Fourteenth Century*.[1] Trevet's commentary is entirely allegorical. Moreover, it is almost certain that Henryson used the *De Genealogia Deorum*[2] of Boccaccio as the source at least of his description of the nine Muses. Boccaccio, it is true, himself uses Fulgentius[3] as a source for the allegorical interpretation of the names of the Muses. But Henryson's poem contains matter unrelated to Fulgentius for which some suggestion may be found in Boccaccio. Boccaccio quotes from the commentary of Macrobius on the *Somnium Scipionis* of Cicero the suggestion that the Muses are to be interpreted as the music of the spheres, 'eas equiparans octo sperarum celi cantibus, nonam volens omnium celorum modulationum esse concentum'.[4] In this he is not followed directly by Henryson, who nevertheless introduces the harmony of the spheres unexpectedly in his account of the wanderings of Orpheus in search of Eurydice (vv. 184–239). Nothing similar appears in Fulgentius, and as we have other evidence to suggest that Henryson knew the *Genealogia*, it seems simplest to assume that here too he used Boccaccio—more particularly when he describes the passage as the 'genealogy' of Orpheus. In the *Genealogia*, Boccaccio, it is well known, attempted to defend classical mythology by a moral interpretation in allegorical terms—a third point which suggests allegorical intention on the part of Henryson.

These sources put the poem in a context very different from that which might have been expected, had the immediate

---

[1] Oxford, 1960. See especially, pp. 58–65.
[2] Ed. V. Romano, 2 vols. (Bari, 1951).
[3] Ed. R. Helm (Teubner, 1898).   [4] XI. ii.

source been directly Augustan—Virgil, for instance, or Ovid. In Boethius the story of Orpheus occurs in the poem (Metrum 12) which ends Book III of *De Consolatione*, and which marks an especial difficulty in the development of the argument. Philosophy has led Boethius to a paradoxical double conclusion, that happiness is the highest good, to be equated with God, and that as God is omnipotent, and yet cannot do evil, evil does not exist. She replies to the incredulity of Boethius with the story of Orpheus, put by her into its appropriate context thus: 'Blisful is that man that may seen the clere welle of good! Blisful is he that mai unbynden hym fro the boondes of the hevy erthe!'[1] Her purpose is at least twofold. On the one hand it is to warn Boethius that if at this stage he abandons his faith in the logical structure of the argument, his fate will be similar to that of Orpheus. More important is the second. Orpheus is one who saw 'the clere welle of good' and unbound himself from the bonds of the heavy earth, as is symbolized by his rescue of Eurydice. But as the concluding lines of the poem indicate, Eurydice has an ambiguous, and even sinister, significance. She is the thought which Orpheus sought to lead to the light above; she is also the desire which turned him back to darkness from the bounds of light. Under both aspects she is explicable in terms of the argument which has preceded.

---

[1] I quote the Chaucerian version (ed. F. N. Robinson, *The Works of Geoffrey Chaucer*, 2nd edit., Boston, 1957, pp. 319–84. All Chaucerian quotations are from this edition). The Latin is (ed. H. F. Stewart, Loeb Classical Library, 1918):

> Felix qui potuit boni
> Fontem uisere lucidum,
> Felix qui potuit gravis
> Terrae soluere uincula.

All direct quotations of Boethius are taken from Stewart's text.

Every man naturally desires the highest good which by the exercise of reason he can attain. At the same time, as a temporal fallen creature, man is subject to illusion. As one who desired the highest good, Orpheus rescued Eurydice. As one subject to illusion, he made the mistake by which he lost her again. The figures of the poem, that is to say, are certainly intended by Boethius to be allegorical.

In his commentary, Trevet analyses the allegory, and because, like St. Thomas Aquinas, he was himself a Dominican friar, he interprets in Thomistic and Aristotelian terms. Orpheus is the *pars intellectiva*, the intellectual power of the soul. Eurydice is the *pars affectiva*, the appetitive power of the soul. Trevet stresses, as Boethius does not, the shepherd Aristaeus, whose pursuit of Eurydice led to her death when she trod on a serpent. The connexion between Aristaeus and Greek ἄριστος, 'best', has probably caused the interpretation of Aristaeus as Virtue, which seeks to be united with the appetitive power of the soul, but from which the appetitive shrinks. In Thomistic terms, that is to say, Aristaeus is moral virtue, as opposed to intellectual or theological virtue—'Not every virtue is a moral virtue, but only those that are in the appetitive power.'[1] The serpent is sensuality, by whose sting Eurydice is given over to the powers of hell, and from which it is within the capability of the intellectual power to rescue her. The monsters of hell symbolize the various dangers which beset the intellectual power in its quest. Cerberus is the world, and his three heads are the three ages—childhood, youth, and old age—during which the worldly man is subject to the death of the spirit. The three Furies are the poten-

---

[1] *Summa Theologica* I–II. LVIII. I.

tiality of sin in thought, word, and deed. Ixion, apparently, is semi-rational human nature, which mistakenly trusts to Fortune, symbolized by the wheel, to win for itself mastery over Nature (Juno). Tantalus is avarice, the root of all evil. Tityos is illegitimate desire to know the future. Orpheus overcomes all these obstructions, only to succumb finally when he is on the very brink of complete success.

Henryson's *moralitas* is enough to show that he accepted this interpretation, but even in his narrative there is evidence to show that he intended Orpheus to represent intellectual, and Eurydice appetitive power. Orpheus, for instance, regards himself as a servant of Venus. Yet in no sense does he win Eurydice; he does not even ask her to marry him. That is the role of the appetitive. Eurydice takes the initiative; it is only after she has offered him her hand that Orpheus becomes a king:

> His noble fame so far it sprang and grew,
> Till at the last the michty quene of Trace,
> Excelland fair, haboundand in richess,
> A message send unto that prince so ying,
> Requyrand him to wed hir and be king.
>
> Euridices this lady had to name;
> And quhene scho saw this prince so glorius,
> Hir erand to propone scho thocht no schame,
> With wordis sueit, and blenkis amorouss,
> Said, 'Welcum, Lord and lufe, schir Orpheuss,
> In this provynce ye salbe king and lord!'
>
> (73–83)

The same point is stressed earlier:

> And mother to the king schir Orpheouss,
> Quhilk throw his wyfe wes efter king of Traiss.
>
> (45–46)

As intellect, Orpheus is divine by descent, but he is sovereign only in so far as Eurydice willingly accepts him. The intellectual power assumes the mastery only at the invitation, and by the consent, of the appetitive. Nor is the mastery more than local and temporary. When Eurydice says to Orpheus

> In this provynce ye salbe king and lord,

the metrical accent falls on 'this'. Orpheus, in other words, is restricted to the realm over which Eurydice has previously ruled, that of appetite and its satisfaction. The worldliness of their married joy is stressed:

> Betuix Orpheuss and fair Erudices,
> Fra thai wer weddit, on fra day to day
> The low of lufe cowth kyndill and incress,
> With mirth, and blythness, solace, and with play
> Off warldly Joy; allace, quhat sall I say?
> Lyk till a flour that plesandly will spring,
> Quhilk fadis sone, and endis with murnyng.
> (85–91)

The death of Eurydice marks the end of Orpheus's kingship:

> My rob ryell, and all my riche array,
> Changit salbe in rude russet and gray,
> My dyademe in till a hate of hair.
> (157–9)

The marriage of Orpheus and Eurydice is worldly, but not vicious: morally, it is precariously neutral. For Orpheus it remains so. When Eurydice is taken from him, he does not know whether to look for her in heaven or in hell. With Eurydice it is different, and the difference first becomes apparent with the change of style in stanza 14. Most of the poem is written in the courtly rhyme-royal of Chaucer and

James, I, but in the first thirteen stanzas the style is that of moral and panegyric rhetoric rather than of courtly love narrative. In stanza 14 the courtly love style briefly appears:

> I say this be Erudices the quene,
> Quhilk walkit furth in to a May mornyng,
> Bot with a madyn, untill a medow grene,
> To tak the air, and se the flouris spring.
>
> (92–95)

Trevet had interpreted the meadow in which Eurydice was killed as *amena presentis vite*. Henryson found a stylistic equivalent of this in the manner of description usual in the poetry of courtly love. Here, as perhaps always in his writings, the use of this style indicates a failure, a worldliness, of moral judgement on the part of the persons described.

When Eurydice walked in the meadow she was bare-footed, and her white shanks were showing. One may perhaps recollect that in Lindsay's *Squyer Meldrum*[1] the Lady of Gleneagles obtained the love of the Squire when she came into his bedroom one May morning,

> Hir schankis quhyte withouttin hois.
>
> (949)

She told her maidens afterwards that she had been walking in her 'Gardine grene':

> (Quod thai) quhair wes ȝour hois and schone:
> Quhy ȝeid ȝe with ȝour bellie bair?
> (Quod scho) the morning wes sa fair:
> For be him that deir Iesus sauld
> I felt na wayis ony maner of cauld.
>
> (1016–20)

[1] Ed. J. Kinsley (London and Edinburgh, 1959).

Henryson only briefly adopts the courtly style, but he puts it in a context strikingly contrasted with that usual in the poetry of courtly love. In the *Knight's Tale* or the *Kingis Quair*, for instance, the May morning serves as background to the courtly lover's first glimpse of his lady and consequent hopeless devotion to her. This for Henryson is the assumed norm of courtly and worldly behaviour. Aristaeus, who sees Eurydice on a May morning, behaves in a way directly opposite. He is a ravisher, whose allegorical function as Virtue is combined with his literal role in a stylistic yoking of apparent incompatibles very characteristic of medieval allegory, and with an effect not dissimilar to that of later metaphysical imagery. The startling combination may well have been regarded by Henryson and his contemporaries as a satisfactory amalgam of wit and imaginative truth.

Henryson took pains to define only to the extent necessary for his allegorical purpose the literal occupation of Aristaeus. Aristaeus is not shepherd, cowherd, or goatherd; he is simply a 'hird' who keeps 'beistis':

> A busteouss hird callit Arresteuss,
> Kepand his beistis, Lay undir a buss.
>   (97–98)

Allegorically, beasts are the carnal passions, the usually uncontrolled appetitive power of the soul, common to beast and man. Henryson exploits the figure in the *Fabillis*:

> Na mervell is, ane man be lyke ane Beist,
> Quhilk lufis ay carnall and foull delyte.
>   (50–51)

As opposed to this, moral virtue is an operative habit (*Summa*

Theologica, I–II. LV. 2) which operates on the appetitive power of the soul, and which therefore is appropriately represented by the herd of beasts, Aristaeus. Eurydice has not come under his control, and is therefore his appropriate prey. When she attempts to escape she at once abandons her position of moral neutrality, the serpent stings her, and she passes from the government of Orpheus to that of the king and queen of hell. With the disappearance of the appetitive, Aristaeus also disappears from the story—and so it may be added, does all possibility of a rescue of Eurydice from hell. Intellect alone is insufficient. As moral virtue, Aristaeus cannot come into direct contact with Orpheus, whose moral neutrality is retained when Proserpina is described to him, not as queen of hell, but as queen of fairy.

Hell is the realm of unsatisfied and uncontrolled appetite. Henryson places there two groups of figures, one traditional since the time of Homer, the other a more medieval list of secular and spiritual rulers. The first is wholly pagan, the second, anachronistically with the characteristic timelessness of poetry and drama in the Middle Ages, part pagan, part Christian. The groups differ, however, not so much in this as in allegorical function; they correspond to different aspects of hell as the place of insatiable, or the place of uncontrolled appetite. The purely pagan group represents failure in satisfaction; the defining factor in the other is not so much the inclusion of Christian figures as the fact that all the figures are rulers, whose government has in some way been unjust or unsuccessful. Jezebel appears, but the masculinity which predominates in Henryson's hell indicates a relevance primarily to Orpheus, the masculine intellect which has failed to bring appetitive power under limitation or control. The distinction of pagan and Christian is also irrelevant in so far as the entire concept is obviously Christian—as Christian as Dante's:

> O dully place, and grundles deip dungeoun,
> Furness of fyre, and stink intollerable,
> Pit of dispair, without remissioun,
> Thy meit wennome, Thy drink is pusonable,
> Thy grit panis and to compte unnumerable;
> Quhat creature cumis to dwell in the
> Is ay deand, and nevirmoir sall de.
>
> (310–16)

The stages of Orpheus's journey to hell's house may be compared with those in the *Lyke-Wake Dirge*:[1]

> When thou from hence away art past,
> *Every nighte and alle,*
> To Whinny-muir thou com'st at last;
> *And Christe receive thy saule.*
>
> If ever thou gavest hosen and shoon,
> Sit thee down, and put them on.
>
> If hosen and shoon thou ne'er gav'st nane,
> The whinnes sall prick thee to the bare bane.
>
> From Whinny-muir when thou may'st pass,
> To Brig o' Dread thou com'st at last.

Tityos lies in the middle of Whinny-muir; the Furies torture Ixion on Brig o' Dread. The pagan insatiable appetites appear in the context of Christian morality, or at least Christian folklore.

---

[1] I quote the version from *The Oxford Book of Ballads*.

Ixion, Tantalus, and Tityos are presented with effective symbolic starkness. Each suffers some aspect of the torture of insatiable appetite; Ixion bound to the wheel of the world; Tantalus thirsting for the water and hungry for the food he cannot reach; Tityos with the vulture tearing his organs of desire—stomach, midriff, heart, liver, and tripes. Each is an aspect of the fallen Eurydice, the pangs of which are only to be quieted by the divine authority of intellect—Orpheus, with the new music which he learned in his journey through the spheres. When Orpheus plays music of this kind, appetite is satisfied. Ixion escapes (significantly, Boethius and most other versions have merely that the wheel stood still): Tantalus drinks: the vulture ceases to gnaw. The success of the narrative as symbol depends on its very abruptness:

> And on his breist thair sat a grisly grip,
> Quhilk with his bill his belly throw can boir,
> Both maw, myddret, hart, lever, and trip
> He ruggit out—his panis was the moir.
> Quhen Orpheus thus saw him suffir soir,
> He tuke his herp and maid sueit melody—
> The grip is fled, and Titius left his cry.
>
> (296–302)

Those who are mentioned in the second list are all rulers—in the first part kings and queens

> Quhilk in thair lyfe full maisterfull had bene,
> And conquerouris of gold, richess, and land.
>
> (319–20)

The catalogue occupies four stanzas (44–47), and the names are so arranged that with each succeeding stanza moral implications become more and more strongly stressed. Hector,

Priam, and Alexander seem to be included (stanza 44) for little reason other than that they were pagan. Antiochus introduces a definite breach of the natural order with his crime of incest. In stanza 45 pagan and Biblical rulers are balanced in alternation; Julius Cæsar, Herod, Nero, Pilate, and Croesus, and the Biblical connotations are the Nativity and Crucifixion. Stanza 46 includes only Old Testament rulers, Pharaoh, Saul, Ahab, and Jezebel, while stanza 47 lists the spiritual rulers of the Christian church who commit offences in the exercise of their power. As has already been noted, Henryson included Jezebel with Eurydice, but it is clear that the stanzas are primarily a catalogue of men who, like Orpheus, have in some way failed in their duty as moral and spiritual leaders.

The poem as we have so far considered it, and as perhaps it most needs to be emphasized, is interior allegorical drama, played with no necessary relevance to the external macrocosm. It would nevertheless be wrong to suppose that Henryson intended his poem to be only a study in analytic moral psychology. Two links, genealogy and music, which as he treats them become almost identical, connect interior drama with exterior universe. The descent of Orpheus from Jupiter represents the descent of human intellect from the divine. Almost equally important is the line—Memory, Apollo, and the Muses—by which Orpheus is able to claim that descent. In particular, his mother is Calliope, 'of all musik maistress', 'finder of all armony'. Among the other Muses, Erato 'drawis lyk to lyk in every thing'; Urania 'is callit armony celestiall'; Clio is 'meditatioun/ Of everything that hes creatioun'. Erato and Urania, that is to say, might be thought of as governing powers in the actual physical universe, while Clio links intellect with creation. With the exception of Polyhymnia, the other Muses function as aspects of the abstract intellect. Polyhymnia is poetry, regarded perhaps as the equivalent in musical speech of external harmony. Her function is described, at least, in terms less abstract than those used of the others.

Traditionally, as I have already pointed out, the nine Muses were associated with the nine celestial spheres—an idea which takes its literary origin from the vision of Er with which Plato concludes his *Republic*.[1] There, it will be remembered, the material universe is the Spindle which turns on the knees of Necessity. Upon each circle stood a Siren who uttered a single note: the combination of notes made up the music of the spheres.

Orpheus is man, musician, and intellectual power, whose function in the microcosm corresponds to that of the Muses in the macrocosm. The relevance of the Muses to the physical universe in which Orpheus exists is brought out by the account of Orpheus's journey through the spheres, during which he does not find Eurydice, but does at least learn some music, the 'armony celestiall' which has already been described as Urania.

> Yit be the way sum melody he lerd.
>
> In his passage amang the planeitis all,
> He hard a hevinly melody and sound,
> Passing all intrumentis musicall,
> Causit be rollyn of the speiris round;

[1] x. 615b et seq.

> Quhilk armony of all this mappamound,
> Quhilk moving seiss unyt perpetuall,
> Quhilk of this warld Plato[1] the saule can call.
>
> (218–25)

Orpheus is the intellectual soul of the microcosm; the harmony of the spheres is the Platonic soul of the macrocosm.

The failure of Orpheus is that in his little world he cannot, and does not attempt to, establish a harmony like that of the spheres. Music is part of his inheritance. When he was born his mother sat him on her knee,

> And gart him souk of hir twa paupis quhyte
> The sueit lecour of all musik perfyte.
>
> (69–70)

The measure of his failure is that between his birth and the death of Eurydice Orpheus is nowhere referred to as a musician. When Eurydice chose him for his fame, stature, and fairness of face, Orpheus remained acquiescent. This is degeneracy.

> It is contrair the Lawis of nature
> A gentill man to be degenerat,
> Nocht following of his progenitour
> The worthe rewll, and the lordly estait.
>
> (8–11)

The degeneracy takes effect in a corresponding degeneracy of his music. After the death of Eurydice, Orpheus leaves the *amena presentis vite* for the forest:

> Him to reioss yit playit he a spring,
> Quhill that the fowlis of the wid can sing,

---

[1] The manuscripts and the Chepman and Myllar print (ed. W. Beattie, Edinburgh Bibliographical Society, 1950) read Pluto, an obvious corruption of Plato. The reference is to the Anima Mundi of the *Timaeus*.

And treis dansit with thair levis grene,
Him to devod from his grit womenting;
Bot all in vane, that wailyeit no thing,
His hairt wes so upoun his lusty quene.

(144–9)

The dancing of the trees is a traditional feature of the legend, exploited by Henryson with particular effectiveness. The trees are the material world, *silva*, brute matter, over which a degenerate music still has some degree of control. Orpheus himself is more than material, and music of the kind he is now capable of producing has no power to make good a loss, which also is more than material, or even to comfort him. The song is musical in the discipline of its stanzaic structure, but the refrain is a question ('Quhair art thow gone, my luve Ewridicess?'), with no answer stated or implied. Within the stanza the normal structure is again question, or imperative appeal—to his harp, to Phoebus, to Jupiter. Where he makes a statement, it is one merely of loss or of change, and when he does attempt resolution, it is at once qualified by the negation of its contrary—a rhetorical device which strengthens rather than weakens the overall negative impression:

Forsuth seik hir I sall,
And nowthir stint nor stand for stok nor stone.

(178–9)

The operative words are those linked by alliteration on *st*—stint, stand, stok, stone.

The appeal to Phoebus and Jupiter indicates the path, not so much to Eurydice as to regeneration, a path which lies through the spheres. Intellectual discipline is the characteristic of the new music which he learns there, a characteristic expressed stylistically, first in the catalogue form of the description, and secondly in the use of the Latin and Greek terms of musical theory.

> Thair leirit he tonis proportionat,
> As duplare, triplare, and emetricus,
> Enolius, and eik the quadruplait,
> Epoddeus rycht hard and curius;
> Off all thir sex, sueit and delicius,
> Rycht consonant fyfe hevinly symphonyss
> Componyt ar, as clerkis can devyse.
>
> Ffirst diatesserone, full sueit, I wiss,
> And dyapasone, semple and dowplait,
> And dyapenty, componyt with the dyss;
> Thir makis fyve of thre multiplicat:
> This mirry musik and mellefluat,
> Compleit and full of nummeris od and evin,
> Is causit be the moving of the hevin.
>
> (219–32)

Some emendation is required. *emetricus* should be *epitritus*: *enolius* should be *emiolius*, and *epoddeus* is for *epogdous*. Granted this, the development of the stanzas is straightforward. The first lists the six arithmetical ratios on which medieval musical theory depended—'proportionat' is Henryson's key word. *duplare* is the ratio 2:1; *triplare* 3:1; *emiolius* (or *sesquialter*) 3:2; *epitritus* (or *sesquitertius*) 4:3; *quadruplait* is 4:1, and *epogdous* is 9:8. With the exception of *epogdous* the ratios are consonant, but *epogdous* corresponds to the musical interval of a tone. The five corresponding musical intervals, 'multiplicait' from the three basic, diapason, diapente, and diatessaron, follow in the second stanza. *duplare* in musical terms is diapason, the interval of an octave. *quadru-plait* is bisdiapason, or double octave. Together these consti-tute 'dyapasone, semple and dowplait'. *emiolius* is diapente, a fifth; *triplare* is diapente and diapason, a double fifth. Together these constitute 'diapenty, componyt with the dyss' ('dyss' perhaps being for disdiapente). *epitritus* is diatessaron, a fourth. In instrumental terms, strings whose lengths were in one of those ratios would produce *consonantia* when struck together.[1]

As narrator, Henryson disclaims any share in the music which he describes:

> Off sic musik to wryt I do bot doit,
> Thairfoir of this mater a stray I lay,
> For in my lyfe I cowth nevir sing a noit.
>
> (240–2)

The remark is to be taken rhetorically rather than personally; the effect is to emphasize the importance of the passage, the only one upon which such comment is made, and it is worth noting that Henryson repeats the effect when he uses Greek terms to describe the harping of Orpheus before Pluto and Proserpina:

> Than Orpheus befoir Pluto sat doun,
> And in his handis quhit his herp can ta,
> And playit mony sueit proportioun,
> With baiss tonis in Ipotdorica,
> With gemilling in Yporlerica.
>
> (366–70)

His music has become 'proportioun'.

[1] See, for instance, Isidore of Seville, *Etymologiae*, III. xiv (ed. W. M. Lindsay, 2 vols., Oxford, 1911), especially the illustrative diagrams, and Boethius, *De Arithmetica* and *De Musica* (J. P. Migne, *Patrologia Latina*, 63, 1079–1300).

The link between Orpheus and Eurydice is love; the allegorical significance of Eurydice is appetite. The more intellectual quality, which also is in greater harmony with the order of the universe, is love. It is this intellectual love which Orpheus learns in his journey through the spheres, and which enables him to rescue Eurydice from hell. Orpheus, however, is not merely intellect, he is fallen intellect, which cannot find its appetite in the heavens at any level. He is therefore always liable to confuse love with appetite, as he did on the brink of hell, and his last words are the cry of the blinded intellect seeking a defintion of its problems.

> Quhat art thow, luve, how sall I the defyne?
> Bittir and sueit, crewall and merciable,
> Plesand to sum, to uthir plent and pyne,
> Till sum constant, to uthir wariable;
> Hard is thy law, thy bandis unbrekable;
> Quho sservis the, thocht thay be nevir so trew,
> Perchance sum tyme thay sall haif causs to rew.
>
> (401–7)

III

THE *TESTAMENT OF CRESSEID*

I stumbled when I saw.
SHAKESPEARE, *King Lear*, IV. i. 19

I

I T is tempting to see in the *Orpheus and Eurydice* the earliest of Henryson's major narratives. The poem has the general characteristics of Henryson's verse—allegorical meaning combined with narrative self-sufficiency—yet at the same time it misses the fullness of human reference which one finds in the *Testament of Cresseid*.[1] In many ways the *Testament* parallels the *Orpheus*, but the figures of Cresseid, Troilus, Calchas, Diomede, even the Lipper Lady, have an immediacy lacking in Aristaeus, Eurydice, and Orpheus. Henryson calls the *Testament* a tragedy, and the word is appropriate in a way which would be impossible in terms of the other poem.

The *Testament* is divided into eight parts. Four of these are narrative: that is to say, they present an account of Cresseid's leprosy and death that is primarily literal. These are to be found in lines 71–140, 344–406, 470–546, and 575 to the end. The other four add no literal detail to the narrative, but

[1] The most important critical studies of the *Testament* are those by E. M. W. Tillyard in *Five Poems 1470–1870* (London, 1948), pp. 5–29, and by A. C. Spearing in *Criticism and Medieval Poetry* (London, 1964), pp. 118–44.

each contributes something of value to its understanding or interpretation. One (1–70) forms a Prologue to the poem; two (407–69 and 547–74) are lyrical comments by Cresseid on her own situation; one (141–343), the vision of the gods, and the sentence passed on Cresseid, is perhaps best interpreted as a representation in allegorical rather than literal terms of the entire early action of the poem. This is the longest single episode, and was therefore, we may perhaps assume, regarded by Henryson as of greatest importance. The eight parts are arranged formally, with a non-narrative episode in each instance followed by a narrative.

Henryson assumed in his readers a knowledge of Chaucer's *Troilus and Criseyde*, and his ironic treatment sometimes depends for its effect on half-hidden references to the events of the longer poem. The *Testament*, however, is in no sense a sequel to the *Troilus*: if one compares the relative sequence of action, Chaucer's still has some way to go, when that of Henryson is completed. In particular, Henryson ignores Chaucer's account of the death of Troilus and the Christian epilogue.

Troilus and Criseyde is the most important extant source for the poem. In addition a relationship to the *Assembly of Gods*, formerly attributed to Lydgate, has been suggested,[1] and Henryson himself refers to 'ane uther quair', apparently as a source for his plot, but in a context so ambiguous and ironic that one can only guess at his intention.[2] For the rest, Henryson

[1] M. W. Stearns, op. cit., pp. 70–72.

[2] See especially B. J. Whiting, 'A Probable Allusion to Henryson's *Testament of Cresseid*', *Modern Language Review*, XL (1945), pp. 46–47. Compare also the notes by J. Kinsley in the *Times Literary Supplement*, 14 November 1952, and by James Gray on 13 March 1953.

used Boccaccio's *De Genealogia Deorum*[1] as a source for the planetary portraits. Boccaccio had brought together an encyclopaedic account of the gods and heroes of classical antiquity; his work included allegorical and astrological interpretations when these seemed relevant. In the past scholars have adduced parallels to Henryson's descriptions from individual, and particularly astrological, works.[2] It has not, I think, previously been noted that most of the astrological and other detail is to be found already combined in Boccaccio. Henryson himself may well have known some of the individual works which Boccaccio quotes, but Boccaccio is certainly his most probable immediate source.

Later in this chapter I discuss some of the divinities in terms of general tradition; here I may perhaps illustrate the direct debt to Boccaccio. As elsewhere, Henryson does not imitate slavishly; he selects and vivifies from a mass of detail those particulars most relevant to the poem as a whole. The portrait of Saturn is based on VIII. i, 'De Saturno', and in particular on the astrological detail which Boccaccio obtained from the *Introductorium* of the Arabic astronomer Albumasar (805–85). The portrait of Jupiter is based on II. ii, 'De Jove primo', and again particularly on the part derived from Albumasar. The portrait of Mars is based on IX. iii, 'De Marte', again with details derived from Albumasar. The portrait of Phoebus is based on IV. iii, 'De Sole', which seems independent of Albumasar. The portrait of Venus, as others have already suggested,[3] belongs largely to the courtly tradition in

[1] See above, Chapter II, p. 28, n. 2.
[2] See especially Tillyard, op. cit., pp. 19–22, and Stearns, op. cit., pp. 73–96.
[3] Stearns, op. cit., pp. 89–92, with the references there cited.

which Venus and Fortune are equated, but it bears clear
enough traces of III. xxii and xxiii, 'De Venere magna' and
'De secunda Venere'. The portrait of Mercury as orator and
poet is based on II. vii, 'De Mercurio primo', and II. xii,
'De Mercurio secundo'; as physician on III. xx, 'De Mercurio
quinto'. The portrait of Cynthia depends more on folklore
and common observation; one may, however, compare
v. ii, 'De Diana'.

Boccaccio's account of Phoebus will serve to illustrate
Henryson's general manner of procedure. Boccaccio is often
euhemeristic; that is to say, he assumes that the pagan divinities were originally human beings who made such an impression on their contemporaries that they were credited with
divine attributes—in the case of the planetary deities, the
attributes of the planets. Thus of Phoebus he says: 'Sane
quoniam hic fere nulla ad hominem spectantia apponi viden-
tur, de Sole planeta loquemur. Finxerunt igitur eum ante
alia regem.' He gives Ovid's description of Sol's palace, of
his chariot with four horses, of his crown and of his many
children. All this, he adds, is properly attributable to the sun.
'Preterea, ut aiunt phylosophi, in rebus procreandis tante
potentie est, ut pater omnis mortalis vite habeatur.' The horses
he connects with the passage of the sun across the sky. 'Nam
Pyrous, qui primus est, pingitur et interpretatur rubeus, eo
quod, primo mane agentibus vaporibus a terra surgentibus,
sol oriens rubeat. Eous, qui secundus est, cum albus effigietur,
dicitur splendidus, eo quod exaltatus iam sol dissolutis vaporibus splendens sit. Ethon autem tertius rubens sed in croceum
tendens, ardens exponitur; nam, sole iam celi medium tenente,
lux eius corusca est et cunctis videtur fervidior. Phegon autem

quartus ex croceo colore tendit in nigrum, et interpretatur terram amans, ostendens, advesperescente die, solem terram petere, id est occasum. Hos tamen equos Fulgentius, esto cum eisdem significationibus, aliter nominat. Videlicet Eritreum, Actheona, Lampos et Phylegeum.'

Henryson's stanzas are:

> As King Royall he raid upon his Chair
> The quhilk Phaeton gydit sum tyme upricht;
> The brichtnes of his face quhen it was bair
> Nane micht behald for peirsing of his sicht.
> This goldin Cart with fyrie bemis bricht
> Four yokkit steidis full different of hew,
> But bait or tyring, throw the Spheiris drew.
>
> The first was soyr, with Mane als reid as Rois,
> Callit Eoye into the Orient;
> The secund steid to Name hecht Ethios,
> Quhitlie and paill, and sum deill ascendent;
> The thrid Peros, richt hait and richt fervent;
> The feird was blak, callit Philologie
> Quhilk rollis Phebus doun into the sey.

$(204-17)$

Henryson, it will be noted, has omitted all euhemeristic references: he has changed the order of the steeds by placing 'Eoye' first—perhaps because he was aware that in Greek ἠώς means 'dawn'.

The details added by Henryson have in general a strikingly visual effect—the chattering teeth and running eyes and nose of Saturn, the foam on the lips of Mars, the dazzling brightness of the face of Phoebus, and the red hood of Mercury.

One other source must be mentioned. The psychology of the meeting between Troilus and Cresseid is basically

Aristotelian, derived from the third book of the *De Anima*, from two (*De Memoria* and *De Somno*) of the treatises which form the *Parva Naturalia* and possibly from Augustine's *De Trinitate* XI. iv.[1]

2

So much by way of preliminary. For the rest one may best approach the *Testament* by analysis of the individual parts and their relationship to each other in terms of theme, imagery, allegory, and style. Prologue and narrative are immediately brought into relationship by the *sententia* with which, in accordance with medieval poetic theory, the *Testament* opens.

> Ane doolie sessoun to ane cairfull dyte
> Suld correspond, and be equivalent.
> (1–2)

Henryson's subject-matter, that is to say, is 'cairfull', and he feels it important that he should describe himself as giving it literary form in a correspondingly 'doolie' season—an immediate indication that he intended his opening description to be relevant, in some sense equivalent, to the entire poem. But the precise equivalence may not at once become clear.

> Richt sa it wes quhen I began to wryte
> This tragedie, the wedder richt fervent,
> Quhen Aries, in middis of the Lent,
> Schouris of haill can fra the north discend,
> That scantlie fra the cauld I micht defend.
> (3–7)

The doolieness is clear enough, but the reader may easily miss the irony with which it is presented. Despite the

---

[1] Stearns, op. cit., pp. 98–105.

commentators, the time intended is not winter but spring; the passage is a variation on the traditional spring opening. Henryson began to write under the zodiacal sign of Aries, the Ram, through which the sun moved between 13 March and 11 April. This is almost the same season as that in which Chaucer made his pilgrims set out for Canterbury, and the literary significance is brought out by the *General Prologue* itself, still more strikingly by one of the best known among the thirteenth-century Harley Lyrics, 'Alysoun'[1]—

> Bytuene Mersh ant Aueril
> when spray beginneþ to springe,
> þe lutel foul haþ hire wyl
> on hyre lud to synge.
> Ich libbe in loue-longinge . . .

So too for the twentieth-century reader, the primary associations of the word Lent may be fasting and penitence. In the fifteenth century, however, the word retained many of its earlier connotations, which were primarily with spring, and so with love. Again the opening of a Harley Lyric may illustrate.[2]—

> Lenten ys come wiþ loue to toune.

The second stanza establishes the background more clearly with the description of the rising of Venus, the planet and goddess of Love, and that of Henryson as himself a courtly lover, standing at the window of his 'oratur' to make his supplication to her deity. The supplication, and the metaphor in which it is expressed, are particularly appropriate to the season of growth.

[1] Ed. G. L. Brook (2nd edit., Manchester, 1956), p. 33.
[2] Ibid., p. 43.

> For I traistit that Venus, luifis Quene,
> To quohome sum tyme I hecht obedience,
> My faidit hart of lufe scho wald mak grene.
>
>   (22–24)

Decay and renewed growth, fading and rejuvenescence—
much of the poem is developed in terms of this metaphor.

To the extent that he makes use of the spring opening,
Henryson's approach is conventional. It is also appropriate,
because the story he has to tell is a tragedy of love. The second
aspect symbolized by the description is the tragic; the season
is a spring which has been blasted until it is almost undistin-
guishable from winter. Venus stands in an astronomically
impossible, but astrologically sinister opposition to Phoebus;
she is clearly visible, but it is only because

> The Northin wind had purifyit the Air
> And sched the mistie cloudis fra the sky.
>
>   (17–18)

The poet is a courtly lover, a servant of Venus, but he is
chilled and old; his prayer for rejuvenescence remains
unanswered. Venus has less power to help him than has the
fire in his chamber, a drink, and Chaucer's *Troilus*. By the
fire, behind his glass window, Henryson half humorously
exemplifies the same opposition of time to love as is found
externally in the brilliance of Venus seen against the hail,
frost and bitter wind of the unseasonable spring.

With himself as crabbed age, Henryson makes a parallel
of the agonized youth of Troilus. His verdict on himself—

> Thocht lufe be hait, yit in ane man of age
> It kendillis nocht sa sone as in youtheid.
>
>   (29–30)

may be contrasted with

> Troilus neir out of wit abraid,
> And weipit soir with visage paill of hew.
> (45–46)

Again the emphasis is on time—youth contrasted with age—and in particular on the changes brought by time—Henryson's common-sense resignation against the alternating hope and despair of the period during which Troilus expected the return of Cresseid to Troy. As has already been mentioned, the reference to Troilus serves also to indicate the period within the saga at which the action of the *Testament* begins —to be precise, after *Troilus* v. 1198, but before v. 1659, the final discovery of Cresseid's faithlessness. A point of Henryson's irony may be indicated here. In Chaucer, it will be remembered, the final discovery comes when Troilus sees the brooch which he had given Cresseid on a *cote-armure* captured by Deiphebus from Diomede—the brooch to which in Henryson's poem, Cresseid refers as she dies.

> O Diomeid, thou hes baith Broche and Belt,
> Quhilk Troylus gave me in takning
> Of his trew lufe—
>
> (589–91)

Henryson makes Cresseid die with these words, and immediately shows by Troilus' utterance, 'Scho was untrew, and wo is me thairfoir', that it was by means of this very brooch that her first faithlessness was already known.

If the disputed[1] reading 'Esperus' of 48 is correct,

> Quhill Esperus rejoisit him againe,

[1] See the note by Bruce Dickins in *The Times Literary Supplement*, 11 December 1924, and by H. Harvey Wood, op. cit., pp. 252–3.

the description of Troilus contains another reference to the
planetary deity of love, seen by Henryson in her position of
evening star. Balanced as the word is against 'wanhope' in
the preceding line, in all probability we must assume a
deliberate pun on the word 'esperance', 'hope', which is
actually the reading of an early print. Chaucer's poem shows
how groundless the hope was; the pun *Esperus/esperance*
indicates the unreliability of Venus, already hinted at in the
failure of the poet's prayer, also addressed to Hesperus, the
evening star, and to be stressed later in the fate of Cresseid,
and the portrait of Venus among the planetary deities:

> . . . all fleschelie Paramour
> Quhilk Venus hes in reull and governance,
> Is sum tyme sweit, sum tyme bitter and sour
> Richt unstabill, and full of variance,
> Mingit with cairfull Joy and fals plesance,
> Now hait, now cauld, now blyith, now full of wo,
> Now grene as leif, now widderit and ago.
>
> (232–8)

The main distinction is that in this portrait Fortune, expressed
by imagery recalling that of the *Moralitas* to *The Taill of the
Paddok and the Mous*, is added to the themes which were
present in the earlier part of the poem—love, time, change,
heat, cold, youth, age, growth, decay.

3

I have already noted that Henryson follows the precepts of
medieval rhetorical theory by opening the *Testament* with a
sententia. A conscious and very individual use of rhetorical
techniques characterizes the whole poem, as indeed should

already be evident from the unconventional use of the conventional spring opening. So too in the references to Chaucer and the 'uther quair' (61), Henryson follows the tradition of citing authorities for the truth of his material, while at the same time his irony prevents him from being the slave of the tradition. Henryson knows that Chaucer and the unknown, perhaps non-existent, author of the 'uther quair' are in no sense authorities for the events of the Trojan War, and also that this, as a matter for critical concern, is unimportant.

> Quha wait gif all that Chauceir wrait was trew?
> Nor I wait nocht gif this narratioun
> Be authoreist, or genyeit of the new
> Be sum Poeit, throw his Inventioun.
>
> (64–67)

The use here for the first time apparently in English[1] of the technical term Invention in a sense which approaches very near to the modern is particularly interesting. Henryson indeed is by way of composing a literary manifesto. Merely by continuing his narrative after such an overture he indicates his opinion of the relative value in poetry of historical fact and invention in the sense which he has given the word. For him poetry self-evidently is more philosophical than history. Strikingly enough, he is prepared to defend his thesis by citing Chaucer's work as a precedent. In a fifteenth-century author this surely proves unusual freedom of mind? In the most Chaucerian of his works, Henryson is not the disciple, rather he regards himself with some justification as a fellow innovator with Chaucer.

Rhetorical also is Henryson's command of aureate diction,

---

[1] See above, Chapter I, *ad. fin.*

the polysyllabic, Latinate style which had such an appeal to fifteenth and early sixteenth-century poets. Here too, however, he stands rather apart. Characteristically, Henryson's diction belongs to the middle or low style; in the *Testament* he makes moderate use of aureation, chiefly to establish contrasts in his level of diction. In the prologue it is mostly to be found in the more conventional parts of the description, and even in those it does not stand alone, but alternates with passages of less conventional monosyllabic utterance, which sometimes at least serve to deflate the pretence of the aureation. Thus, Henryson's wish as a courtly lover to pray to Venus is presented in aureate terms:

> And therupon with humbill reverence,
> I thocht to pray hir hie Magnificence.
>
> (25–26)

Everyday existence breaks back with the monosyllables of the next line:

> Bot for greit cald as than I lattit was.

So in the description of the season there is a similar ironic conflict between the Latinity of 'Aries', 'fervent', 'discend', 'defend', and the English 'schouris of haill' and 'scantlie fra the cauld'. There is also the humorous use of scientific language to present a very ordinary fact:

> To help be Phisike quhair that nature faillit
> I am expert, for baith I have assailit.
>
> (34–35)

In other words, because Henryson felt cold, he sat down at the fire with a drink. This process is technically the reverse of that described above; in the one a monosyllabic, in the other a polysyllabic diction, gives the half-humorous impression of earthly reality. In both the everyday is stressed at the expense of the ideal and the inflated.

The last point, perhaps, that need be noted in this discussion of Henryson's rhetoric is his elaborate and skilful use of alliteration. Heavy alliteration is of course characteristic of much late medieval poetry written in Scotland and the north of England; the cause may be the vigorous survival of alliterative verse on the Old English pattern in the north and west. It is in accordance with this that Henryson has, for instance, a marked tendency to join the beginning with the end of a line by alliterating syllables. As this is sometimes disguised by the spelling, it is important that the reader should judge by ear rather than by the appearance on the printed page. The pattern of the first line, with the first and last stressed syllables alliterating on *d*, is clear enough:

> Ane *d*oolie sessoun to ane cairfull *d*yte

The initial *k* sound of *cairfull* then becomes the link joining the beginning and end of the second line:

> Suld *c*orrespond, and be e*qu*ivalent.

First and second lines together are joined by the emergence of a subsidiary initial sound in the first as the main alliterative link of the second. The third line is held together by alliteration on *r*:

> *R*icht sa it wes quhen I began to *wr*yte.

The third, in turn, is linked to the fourth and fifth by a pattern of *r*'s, which includes the repetition of the word *richt*

> This t*r*agedie, the wedde*r r*icht fe*r*vent,
> Quhen A*r*ies, in middis of the Lent.

The pattern of the final couplet is the most elaborate of all. The beginning and end of the sixth line are linked by *s* sounds; in phonetic terms, [ʃ] and [s].

> *Sch*ouris of haill can fra the north di*s*cend

Superimposed on this is the sequence *s*, *k*, *d*, which is repeated in the seventh line:

> *Sch*ouris of haill *c*an fra the north *d*iscend,
> That *s*cantlie fra the *c*auld I micht *d*efend.

It is probable that Henryson also meant to exploit the eye-alliteration of the initial letters in *schouris* and *scantlie*.

The stanza follows the rhyme-pattern ababbcc ('rhyme royal'), and there is a kind of harmony between the b-rhymes in *ent* and the c-rhymes in *end*. The sole difference—that the final *t* is a voiceless, the final *d* a voiced alveolar stop—is sufficient to preserve the similarity of the rhyming syllables, without (to my ear) harshness or monotony.

To analyse every stanza in this way would be tedious, but a few further examples must be quoted. The sixth and seventh lines of the second stanza are linked by patterned alliteration similar to that at the end of the first stanza; the *g* and *f* of *goldin face* are repeated in *God Phebus*; monotony is avoided by the fact that in line six Henryson has a disyllable *goldin* followed by a monosyllable *face*, whereas in line seven a monosyllable *God* is followed by the disyllable *Phebus*; secondly by the heavy alliteration on *d* ('direct discending doun') with which the stanza closes. This last also serves as a kind of echo-link to the first stanza, which ends with the rhyme and alliteration of *discend* and *defend*.

Line 19 clearly falls into two parts, each introduced by *the*:

The froist freisit, the blastis bitterly.

The consonant sequence of the first part is *th*, *frst*, *frst*; that of the second is *th*, *bl(s)t(s)*, *bt(r)l*: in the first part, that is to say, we have a repeated identical sequence of sounds; in the second, one almost identical, with *b*, *l*, and *t* appearing in both subdivisions, and the additional sounds, *s* and *r*, prominent in the pattern of the beginning of the line.

I have already commented on the aureate diction in lines 25–26:

And thereupon with humbill reverence,
I thocht to pray hir hie Magnificence.

But Henryson is not content with aureation alone. The contrast between poet and goddess is stressed by the alliteration of *humbill* and *hie*, occurring as it does in identical syllables of successive lines. The contrast is strengthened by the opposition of disyllable to monosyllable, and by the contrast between the stressed back vowel of *humbill* and the high front vowel of *hie*.

Line 51 makes elaborate play on *t*, *r*, and *s*, and incidentally links the beginning with the end of the line by alliteration on *t*:

*Tr*ais*t*ing *t*o *Tr*oy that *scho s*uld mak *ret*our.

4

The first narrative episode of the *Testament* (lines 71–140) is most obviously linked to the prologue by parallelism of incident. In the Prologue, Henryson in his oratory makes a prayer to Venus; in the episode, Cresseid makes a prayer to

Venus and Cupid in the oratory of the temple where her father is priest. (Calchas's character in the main narrative rather closely resembles that of Henryson as presented in the Prologue.) But the similarity goes further. Nothing in the episode, it might be said, corresponds immediately to the description of the blasted spring. Already in the Prologue, however, this description was used metaphorically. Henryson's trust, when he prayed to Venus, was that

> My faidit hart of lufe scho wald mak grene
>
> (24)

He is not rewarded; the failure in his own heart parallels the external failure of spring. It is this aspect of the description that is taken up by the first, as by later, episodes of the narrative. Cresseid is a flower:

> O fair Creisseid, the flour and A per se
> Of Troy and Grece.
>
> (78–79)

The divine promise had been that she should be the flower of love:

> Ye gave me anis ane devine responsaill
> That I suld be the flour of luif in Troy.
>
> (127–8)

Untimely frost has blasted that promise

> Ye causit me alwayis understand and trow
> The seid of lufe was sawin in my face,
> And ay grew grene throw your supplie and grace.
> Bot now allace that seid with froist is slane,
> And I fra luifferis left and all forlane.
>
> (136–40)

The metaphoric continuity with the Prologue is plain.

But the comparison of the poet's treatment of himself and of Cresseid brings out differences as well as parallels. In a sense, Henryson's situation in the Prologue is natural and inevitable; he is 'ane man of age', whose green has faded rather than been blasted. Fire, drink, and Chaucer bring him the pleasure he no longer obtains from love. He is contrasted, not only with the spring, but also with Cresseid, whose flower has been blasted by untimely and unnatural frost. Indeed, at first glance, there is even something more than a little puzzling about the metaphor used by Cresseid. She is a young woman; so far there has been no mention of the leprosy from which she dies; none the less, to say that the seed of love sown in her face has been slain by frost, at once suggests some physical change in her beauty. The whole narrative at this point implies that to herself Cresseid is already altered and physically disfigured. She does not say that she has deserted Troilus and been deserted by Diomede; rather

> I fra Diomeid and Nobill Troylus
> Am clene excludit, *as abject odious*.
>
> (132–3)

She keeps from the sight of others, both on her journey to Calchas's mansion and during the sacrifice in the Temple. Even her anger against Venus and Cupid seems better motivated if one regards her as already in some sense conscious of the ravaging disease from which she is to die.

From whatever point of view the *Testament* is considered, one must, I think, assume that Cresseid's leprosy is to be regarded as the punishment for her 'brukkilnes', her lightness in love. (I shall discuss the question of her blasphemy later.) Venus and Cupid are the deities of love: in Cresseid's dream-vision, as I hope to show, the deities as a group are to be regarded as embodiments of the general principles which govern most aspects of human and earthly affairs. To this extent Henryson is a Platonist or neo-Platonist who considers what might to others seem abstractions as the controlling realities of the world. Venus and Cupid, therefore, are Love in a very real sense, powers with established laws of their own, against which Cresseid has offended—again in a very real sense, because the offence has its own retribution in the form of a killing disease, leprosy, which Henryson clearly regarded as some form of venereal affliction. From this point of view, the critical stage in her story is not so much her abandonment of Troilus, nor her abandonment by Diomede, as the episode to which Henryson devotes little more than a single stanza— her life as a prostitute in the 'Court commoun'. Significantly, it is at this point that the image of Cresseid as the flower first appears, and in such a context as to make it pretty clear that the beginning of the blight that killed the flower is to be found in the 'Court commoun':

> O fair Creisseid, the flour and A per se
> Of Troy and Grece, how was thou fortunait!
> To change in filth all thy Feminitie,
> And be with fleschlie lust sa maculait,
> And go amang the Greikis air and lait
> Sa giglotlike, takand thy foull plesance!
> I have pietie thou suld fall sic mischance.
>
> (78–84)

The emphasis here is on change, and the manner in which it is obtained is one of the triumphs of Henryson's controlled and powerful use of alliteration. The stanza is bound together by the repetition of the sound *f*, to which is subordinated *l*. The key words begin with *f*. In the first line they are *fair* and *flour*, words with no immediately unpleasant or tragic overtones, beyond the fact that the fairness of flowers, like human love, is traditionally short-lived:

> Nec meum respectet, ut ante, amorem,
> qui illius culpa cecidit, uelut prati
> ultimi flos, praetereunte postquam
>   tactus aratro est.[1]

In Henryson's line, however, it is the flower-like beauty of Cresseid that is stressed. The change begins with *fortunait* in the next line, in itself a neutral word, but one which implies change, which in context must clearly be for the worse. The change is defined in the next lines; it is from *feminitie* to *filth* by way of the *flesh*; the *l* sound which has been subordinate in *flour*, *filth*, and *fleschlie* is dominant in *lust* and appears in *maculait*, which in turn has contrasting overtones of the Immaculate Virgin. *Foull*, strengthened as it is by the assonance of *fall* in the last line, concludes the transformation. Semantically, it is the complete reverse of *fair*, and phonetically it contains both the *f* and the *l* sound. *Giglotlike*, an unusual word brought into further prominence by the subordinate *g* alliteration in *go* and *Greikis*, stresses the background of harlotry against which the whole development is to be seen.

Henryson nowhere returns directly to Cresseid's harlotry, and she herself (in naturalistic terms, not unnaturally) does not allude to it, either in conversation with her father, or in

[1] C. J. Fordyce (ed.), *Catullus* (Oxford, 1961), XI. 21–24.

her outcry against Venus and Cupid. But, as I have already
stressed, the *Testament* is to be read on two levels of meaning,
the literal and the allegorical or symbolic. To Henryson the
allegorical is the more important, but as in all good medieval
allegory, the figurative sense is solidly based on the literal.
Cresseid's life as a harlot, and the attitude of mind which led
to that life, form the literal foundation of the allegorical
structure of the *Testament*.

The attitude is still present in her charge against Venus
and Cupid. Again, one may compare Henryson's self-portrait.
In the Prologue he prays for an impossibility—that his old
age should be turned into youth—but his at least is a prayer
rather than a demand, and when he receives no answer, he is
capable of making a virtue of necessity. This stands completely
opposed to Cresseid's attitude in the early part of the poem.
She does not pray, she demands and assumes that natural law
should be set aside for her benefit. Cresseid's belief in her own
perpetual youth and beauty, her assumption that

> The seid of lufe was sawin in my face,
> And ay grew grene throw your supplie and grace,

is contradicted by all experience of time and change. Her
prostitution likewise ignores the inevitability of change, in
particular, change brought about by disease. So, her outcry
against Venus, 'Thy Mother, of lufe the blind Goddes', is
based, not on experience, but the same false philosophy of
existence. Henryson stresses, and Cresseid eventually admits,
that given the conduct of Cresseid, her leprosy was inevitable;
at this stage of the poem, however, she regards it as the blind
blow of an essentially malignant fate. This attitude of mind,

and the conduct which it entails, Henryson regards as blasphemy; it is this to which Cupid returns in his speech before the gods:

> Saying of hir greit Infelicitie
> I was the caus, and my Mother Venus,
> Ane blind Goddes, hir cald, that micht not se,
> With sclander and defame Injurious;
> Thus hir leving unclene and Lecherous
> Scho wald returne on me and my Mother.
>
> (281–6)

In this context it should be noticed that part of the advice given to Cresseid by the Lipper Lady is 'I counsall the mak vertew of ane neid' (478), and that Cresseid eventually declares 'Nane but my self as now I will accuse' (574).

5

The obvious allegory of the *Testament* is concentrated in the second non-narrative episode, Cresseid's dream-vision of the planetary deities, and the sentence passed by them on her *brukkilnes* and blasphemy. One may say that in themselves lines 141–343 form a traditional dream-allegory of a type which elsewhere Henryson only approaches in the Prologue to *The Taill of the Lyon and the Mous*; an allegory which incorporates material similar to that of *Orpheus and Eurydice*, and which was to some extent directly modelled on the *Prologue* to Chaucer's *Legend of Good Women*. Like Chaucer, Henryson narrates the trial of a heretic who had blasphemed against the God of Love—and it is perhaps of some importance that one of Chaucer's principal heresies was his presentation

of Criseyde in *Troilus and Criseyde*. Nevertheless, the similarity is no more than general. More important is the correspondence with Henryson's own *Orpheus and Eurydice*, a
correspondence which may be considered under two heads.
Allegorically, and in terms of narrative, Eurydice corresponds to Cresseid—it is almost as if one had been a preliminary sketch for the other. The resemblance includes, but is
not limited to, verbal detail.

> Till at the last Erudices he knew,
> Lene and deidlyk, and peteouss paill of hew,
> Rycht warsche and wane, and walluid as the weid,
> Hir Lilly lyre wes lyk unto the leid.
>
> Quod he, 'My lady leill, and my delyt,
> ffull wo is me to se yow changit thus;
> Quhair is your rude as ross with cheikis quhyte,
> Your cristell ene with blenkis amorus,
> Your Lippis reid to kiss delicius?'
>
> (*O. and E.* 348–56)

Compare the resemblance with a difference in the meeting
of Troilus with Cresseid:

> And nevertheless not ane ane uther knew.
>
> (518)

Earlier, we have Calchas:

> He luikit on hir uglye Lipper face,
> The quhilk befor was quhyte as Lillie flour.
>
> (372–3)

Cresseid exploits the same *ubi sunt* motif as Orpheus:

> Quhair is thy Chalmer wantounlie besene?
>
> (416)

Identical physical details are stressed:

> Thy Cristall Ene minglit with blude I mak.
> (337)

> Yit than hir luik into his mynd it brocht
> The sweit visage and amorous blenking
> Of fair Cresseid sumtyme his awin darling.
> (502–4)

Clearly enough, there is a close verbal resemblance between
the description of Eurydice in Hell and that of Cresseid as a
leper. (The greater realism and pathos of the *Testament*
might seem to suggest that it is the later.) But the correspondence is more than verbal. Allegorically, Eurydice represents
non-intellectual appetite, concerned only with immediate
satisfaction, and damned when she deliberately tries to
escape the domination of moral virtue (Aristaeus). Much the
same is to be said of Cresseid, and Henryson's diction indicates that in fact he had made this judgement, and thought in
these terms:

> Quhen Diomeid had all his appetyte,
> And mair, fulfillit of this fair Ladie.
> (71–72)

> And go amang the Greikis air and lait
> Sa giglotlike, takand thy foull plesance!
> (82–83)

In itself, it will be remembered, appetite is morally neutral;
but to attain moral excellence, the government of Reason
(Orpheus) and Moral Virtue (Aristaeus) must be applied.
Whether one judges the poem on realistic or allegorical terms,
Henryson pities Cresseid because he realizes these lost moral

potentialities. Her life in the Court commoun shows her rejection of moral virtue; as has already been indicated, her outcry against Venus and Cupid—

> O fals Cupide, is nane to wyte bot thow,
> And thy Mother, of lufe the blind Goddes!
>
> (134–5)

shows her rejection of Reason. One might perhaps recollect that in the *Orpheus and Eurydice* Henryson indicates the same process by a brief adoption of the diction characteristic of the poetry of courtly love—poetry of which, in English, *Troilus* was the supreme example.

All this is preliminary to the dream-vision in the *Testament*, a preliminary necessary if one is to read the vision in the appropriate way. But there is another and more direct parallel between *Orpheus and Eurydice* and the *Testament*. When Orpheus sets out to look for Eurydice, it is among the planets that he first looks for her:

> Quhen endit wer thir songis lamentable,
> He tuk his harp and on his breist can hing,
> Syne passit to the hevin, as sayis the fable,
> To seik his wyfe, bot that welyeid no thing:
> By Wedlingis Streit he went but tareing,
> Syne come doun throw the speir of Saturne ald,
> Quhilk fadir is to all the stormis cald.
>
> Quhen scho wes socht outhrow that cauld regioun,
> Till Jupiter his grandschir can he wend,
> Quhilk rewit soir his Lamentatioun,
> And gart his spheir be socht fro end to end;
> Scho was nocht thair; and doun he can descend
> Till Mars, the god of battell and of stryfe,
> And socht his spheir, yit gat he nocht his wyfe.

Than went he doun till his fadir Phebus,
God of the sone, with bemis brycht and cleir;
Bot quhen he saw his awin sone Orpheuss
In sic a plicht, that changit all his cheir,
And gart annone ga seik throw all his spheir;
Bot all in vane, his lady come nocht thair:
He tuk his leif and to Venus can fair.

Quhen he hir saw, he knelit and said thuss:
'Wait ye nocht weill I am your awin trew knycht?
In luve none leler than Schir Orpheuss;
And ye of luve goddass, and most of micht,
Of my lady help me to get a sicht.'
'fforsur,' quod scho, 'ye mone seik nedirmair.'
Than fra Venus he tuk his leif but mair.

Till Mercury but tary is he gone,
Quhilk callit is the god of eloquens,
Bot of his wyfe thair gat he knawlege none.
With wofull hairt he passit doun from thens;
On to the mone he maid no residens:
Thus from the hevin he went onto the erd,
Yit be the way sum melody he lerd.

(184–218)

The planets, and the music of the spheres produced by their movement, stand to the universe in the same relationship as that which should ideally exist between Orpheus and Eurydice, Reason and Appetite. They represent law and government, against which Eurydice has rebelled. Eurydice as a consequence is not to be found in their realm.

And to the hevin he passit up belyfe,
Schawand to us the Lyfe contemplatyfe,
The perfyte wit, and eik the fervent luve

> We suld haif allway to the hevin abuve;
> Bot seildin thair our appetyte is fundin,
> It is so fast within the body bundin.
>
> (447–52)

In the *Testament* the significance of the planets is almost precisely the same. They represent one aspect of the moral, but also, and perhaps primarily, the physical law of the universe, a law which is most clearly expressed for the twentieth-century reader by such terms as time and change, growth and decay. At the same time, they form the link between the metaphor of the blasted spring discussed above, and the clear moral perception of the poem. Cresseid's offence is twofold. She has outraged the moral as well as the physical laws of the universe. Punishment for any breach of the physical laws is final and inevitable. That for a breach of the moral law is inevitable, but need not, save in physical terms, be final. The dream-vision is of the judgement and punishment of Cresseid for both sides of her offence.

Cresseid has failed to realize her limitations as a creature, in Henryson's phrase a 'thing generabill'. The deities are introduced in terms of this idea—the seven planets

> Quhilk hes power of all thing generabill
> To reull and steir be thair greit Influence,
> Wedder and wind, and coursis variabill.
>
> (148–50)

They are the powers against whom Cresseid's conduct has offended, and by whom therefore she is judged and punished. In themselves they are neither friendly nor hostile; they are the indifferent laws of the universe. The difference in emotional appeal results from a difference of function, which entails that some should appear more favourable to human beings than others. In fact, as Henryson presents them, they fall rather neatly into two classes, the 'hostile' powers, Saturn, Mars, the ambiguous Venus, and the Moon, alternating with the 'favourable', Jupiter, Apollo, and Mercury. Each presents some aspect of the government of 'all thing generabill', and so has some relevance to the fate of Cresseid. The final judgement, however, is left to the highest and lowest power, both hostile, Saturn and the Moon.

In terms of medieval cosmology, the sphere proper to 'all thing generabill' lay beneath the moon. In the realm of the planets, everything was eternal, but at the same time linked in the great chain of being with things and events in the mortal world beneath. From the terrestrial point of view, everything that happened in the natural course of events was directly governed by the single or combined action of the planets. So too earth was regarded under two separate aspects; from one point of view as the home of 'all thing generabill', and from the other of everything corruptible. (Earth, as the central point of the material universe, was therefore necessarily the furthest removed from God.) According to the aspect stressed, there was a tendency to one or another of two semi-religious philosophies; the naturalistic Platonism of Chartres emphasizing generation; the Gnostic emphasizing corruption. Henryson's phrase relates him to the school of Chartres, but in fact Gnostic elements, probably derived from astrological treatises and Macrobius's commentary on the *Somnium Scipionis*, are by no means lacking in the planetary portraits. Saturn primarily represents the Gnostic, Jupiter the Platonic element; the others are best understood in terms of these two.

Saturn is first, and to illustrate his position I may perhaps quote from Gilbert Murray's *Five Stages of Greek Religion*:[1]

'The various Hermetic and Mithraic communities, the Naasenes described by Hippolytus, and other Gnostic bodies, authors like Macrobius and even Cicero in his *Somnium Scipionis*, are full of the influence of the seven planets and of the longing to escape beyond them. For by some simple psychological law the stars which have inexorably pronounced our fate, and decreed, or at least registered the decree, that in spite of all striving we must needs tread their prescribed path; still more perhaps the Stars who know in the midst of our laughter how that laughter will end, become inevitably powers of evil rather than good, beings malignant as well as pitiless, making life a vain thing. And Saturn, the chief of them, becomes the most malignant. To some of the Gnostics he becomes Jaldaboath, the Lion-headed God, the evil Jehovah. The religion of later antiquity is overpoweringly absorbed in plans of escape from the prison of the seven planets.'

Murray might almost have been writing with Cresseid's 'Allace that ever I maid you Sacrifice' (126) and the portrait of Saturn in mind.

There is, however, a relationship between the idea of Saturn held by Henryson and late antiquity closer even than that of emotional tone. Saturn was chief of the planets as a result not merely of his astronomically outermost position, but also of the allegorical interpretation given to his name and legend. Saturn in Greek is Kronos (*Κρόνος*); this was

---

[1] (London, 1935), pp. 146–7. Compare also Chaucer, *Knight's Tale*, III. 2461–2.

early identified with the word Chronos ($X\rho\acute{o}\nu os$), 'Time'. The legend that Saturn devoured his own children was taken as an allegory of Time devouring his sons.[1] Time as opposed to eternity was proper to the lower world; Saturn therefore was chief power over the lower world. As Father Time he was inevitably portrayed as a being of immense age, and it is this aspect which Henryson regards as dominant:

> His face fronsit, his lyre was lyke the Leid,
> His teith chatterit, and cheverit with the Chin,
> His Ene drowpit, how sonkin in his heid,
> Out of his Nois the Meldrop fast can rin.
>
> (155–8)

Saturn here is almost more Old Age than Time. But his character as Time is not forgotten. He 'gave to Cupide litill reverence' (152). Time, in other words, has small respect for individual love or desire.

> Ane busteous bow within his hand he boir,
> Under his girdill ane flasche of felloun flanis,
> Fedderit with Ice, and heidit with hailstanis.
>
> (166–8)

Time's weapons kill with cold. The emphasis on winter and cold throughout links portrait with Prologue and with the metaphor of the blasted spring. Saturn is the power who blasts spring.

Platonic is not the word that immediately suggests itself to the modern reader of the Chartres Platonists. Modern studies of Plato concern themselves so much with the theory of Ideas, the political system of the *Republic*, or even the

[1] See, for instance, Cicero, *De Nat. De.* II. xxv. 64, 65; Isidore, *Etymologiae*, VII. 31.

relation between Platonic and Socratic, that it comes as something of a shock to discover how much medieval Platonism concerned itself with the physical world of generation and decay. This is partly because to most modern readers the *Timaeus* is less familiar than the *Republic* or *Symposium*, but in fact the *Timaeus*, in the fourth-century translation of Chalcidius, was the only authentic work of Plato available to medieval scholars and poets of western Europe. With this too had been combined a good deal of Neo-Platonic and non-Platonic material, for example, the works of Pseudo-Dionysius with the commentary often attributed to Maximus the Confessor, and the works of Apuleius, which were then taken to include the *Asclepius*. The end-product may be exemplified by the *De Mundi Universitate* of Bernardus Sylvestris, which E. R. Curtius rather unfairly describes as 'a mixture of cosmological speculation with the praise of sexuality'.[1] C. S. Lewis is more perceptive[2] when he speaks of the sanity with which, at the conclusion of his work, Bernardus speaks of the male sexual organs. He describes their function under a double metaphor; they rebuild Nature, and they are the weapons in the fight against chaos and death.

> Saecula ne pereant decisaque cesset origo
> Et repetat primum massa soluta chaos;
> Cum morte invicti pugnant genialibus armis,
> Naturam reparant perpetuantque genus.

It is in this tradition that the portrait of Jupiter in the *Testament* must be seen. Henryson stresses that Jupiter is

[1] Curtius, op. cit., p. 112. The entire chapter is important for the present argument.

[2] *Allegory of Love* (Oxford, 1936), p. 97.

Saturn's son. I should not care to press the point too far, but he may well mean that Jupiter's generative function only exists in the realm of Saturn, that is to say, in time. Saturn is the destructive power; Jupiter the

> Nureis to all thing generabill,
> Fra his Father Saturne far different.
>
> (171–2)

The repetition of 'all thing generabill' from 148 doubly stresses the point. He is the god of the unblasted spring who wears

> Upon his heid ane Garland, wonder gay,
> Of flouris fair, as it had bene in May.
>
> (174–5)

But most clearly in the tradition of Bernard is the description of Jupiter's weapons:

> And burelie brand about his midill bair;
> In his richt hand he had ane groundin speir,
> Of his Father the wraith fra us to weir.
>
> (180–2)

Saturn is Time; his wrath is Time's destructive power. The phallic symbolism of his son and opponent's weapons is obvious, as is also the relationship of that symbolism to the concluding metaphor of Bernard's *De Mundi Universitate*. For Henryson, as for Bernard, generation is the only temporal protection against the condition of temporality.

The contrast between the two deities is maintained by the contrast in style and level of diction used for the descriptions. That of Saturn is composed in low style, and a vocabulary which is deliberately harsh and colloquial. To my ear the key words are *busteous, churle, crabitlie, fronsit, chatterit, cheverit, drowpit, Meldrop, bla, Iceschoklis, lyart, felterit, ouirfret, busteous,* and *flasche.* The portrait of Jupiter employs a more obviously melodious and generally Latinate diction, which gains much from such words as *amiabill, Starnis, Firmament, Nureis, generabill, burelie, Garland, flouris, May, Cristall, goldin, garmound,* and *grene.* In the description of Saturn there are thirteen finite verbs, only two of which are parts of the verb 'to be'. The description of Jupiter contains six, of which four belong to the verb 'to be', and one other belongs to the verb 'to have'. The first stanza of the Jupiter portrait contains only one finite verb, which significantly is to be found in a subordinate clause. Not only, that is to say, is the level of diction higher in the second portrait, but the style is more static, the movement more formal, less vivid. The associations of the words used to describe Jupiter are certainly with spring, growth and procreation, but the style and syntax are decorative rather than vigorous. The portrait of Saturn is by far the more powerful. Jupiter must be described to preserve the completeness of Cresseid's universal vision, but it is in such a way as to throw into bolder relief the portrait of Saturn. The emphasis is on Saturn.

A somewhat similar contrast sets off the portraits of the friendly against those of the hostile deities in general. Particularly interesting is the comparison of the portrait of Mars with those of Apollo and Mercury. Mars is described in such words as *roustie, glowrand, bullar, tuitlyeour, brag*: Apollo in melodious diction like that used of Jupiter—*Lanterne, Lamp, Nureis, Influence, Spheiris, Orient, ascendent, fervent,* and the proper names *Phebus, Phaeton, Eoye, Ethios, Peros, Philologie.*

This again contrasts with the still Latinate, but somewhat lower and more professional diction used in the description of Mercury, who is the patron of activities belonging to a less exalted sphere. As a consequence, the diction of this portrait might be described as middle: most obviously so in such lines as

> His Hude was reid, heklit atouir his Croun,
> Lyke to ane Poeit of the auld fassoun.
>
> (244–5)

or

> Honest and gude, and not ane word culd le.
>
> (252)

The diction is not appreciably higher, despite the more professional vocabulary of

> Boxis he bair with fine Electuairis,
> And sugerit Syropis for digestioun,
> Spycis belangand to the Pothecairis,
> With mony hailsum sweit Confectioun.
>
> (246–9)

This, nevertheless, is more than sufficient to distinguish the portrait from that of Cynthia which follows.

The portrait of Venus stands somewhat apart. The vocabulary is certainly that of courtly poetry, and by her very function Venus has a connexion with generation and growth. The diction thus has affinities with that of the portraits of Jupiter and Apollo. But the distinctive feature of the style is the careful balancing of unreconciled opposites:

> The ane half grene, the uther half Sabill black.
>
> (221)

or

> Quhyles perfyte treuth, and quhyles Inconstance.
>
> (224)

or

> Under smyling scho was dissimulait.
>
> (225)

or

> Mingit with cairfull Joy and fals plesance.
>
> (246)

The emphasis in fact is on ambiguity, and the rhetorical tradition in which the portrait is to be placed is that of the courtly complaint against Fortune, such as is to be found in Chaucer's *Book of the Duchess*:

> Hir moste worshippe and hir flour ys
> To lyen, for that ys hyr nature:
> Withoute feyth, lawe, or mesure
> She ys fals; and ever laughynge
> With oon eye, and that other wepynge . . .
> She ys th'envyouse charite.
>
> (630–4, 642)

The *Book of the Duchess* certainly is very early Chaucer, but it is perhaps worth noting how much more assured and powerful Henryson is in his use of the rhetorical tradition.

In one respect the portrait of Saturn stands apart from that of any other deity. I have already commented both on the number of finite verbs used in his portrait, and on the comparative scarcity among them of such static descriptive verbs as 'be' and 'have'. Several of the key words already singled out are verbs—for instance, *chatterit*, *cheverit*, *drowpit*, *rin*, *out woir*. This is true of none of the other portraits. In them nouns, adjectives, and participles are the dominant words. The result is the impression of power and energy which one gains from the portrait of Saturn; he is undoubtedly the pre-eminent divinity; the reader expects victory for him rather than any other power in the debate that follows. He does not speak in the actual debate, but it is he with the subordinate Cynthia who pronounces sentence finally on Cresseid.

If one attempts to classify the deities in terms of their respective leaders, Saturn and Jupiter, Mars is dissension, War, the mad ally of destructive Time; Phoebus the main agent of the procreative process, an agent, however, whose own subjection to Time is stressed by the emphasis laid on his rising and setting in the description of the four horses. With Jupiter there is no morning or evening; the horses of Phoebus are the condition of his function and existence:

> The first was soyr, with Mane als reid as Rois,
> Callit Eoye into the Orient;
> The secund steid to Name hecht Ethios,
> Quhitlie and paill, and sum deill ascendent;
> The thrid Peros, richt hait and richt fervent;
> The feird was blak, callit Philologie
> Quhilk rollis Phebus doun into the sey.
>
> (211–17)

Venus provides some kind of link between Saturn and Jupiter. Her connexion with procreation is obvious, and to that extent she is Jupiter's feminine equivalent. This is indicated by the greenness of her dress, symbolizing that 'all fleschelie Paramour' is 'now grene as leif', and her golden hair, which correspond to the green and gold of Jupiter's dress and hair, and so to the green and gold of spring. But the green is only partial. Half her dress is 'Sabill black', because 'fleschelie Paramour' is soon 'widderit and ago'. The relevance of this is not to Cresseid alone, but general. Compare the metaphor in Henryson's own unsuccessful prayer to Venus. Venus belongs ultimately to the party of Saturn. Generation, one might say, assures immortality only to the race: 'fleschelie Paramour', as represented by the individual Henryson or Cresseid, remains mortal.

Apollo and Venus each receive three stanzas of description, as contrasted with the usual two (Saturn has two and a half, Cynthia one and a half). This corresponds to the supreme importance of these two deities for the individual, and at the same time echoes the opposition of the two already present in the imagery of the Prologue:

> And fair Venus, the bewtie of the nicht,
> Uprais, and set unto the west full richt
> Hir goldin face in oppositioun
> Of God Phebus direct discending doun.
>
> (11–14)

Mercury, as Rhetoric, with which is included Poetry, is plainly suited to be Speaker of the divine assembly. On his divine plane he corresponds to Henryson and Chaucer on the human, and he is described in terms very similar to those used of Aesop in the *Fabillis*. As god of Medicine he is perhaps best regarded as a temporary bulwark against the forces of decay—for Cresseid a bulwark that will be totally ineffective.

Cynthia, as almost always in medieval poetry, represents Change.

The reader will notice that neither Jupiter nor Apollo, whom one might regard as Cresseid's natural protectors, plays any part in the debate. In terms of the allegory, Poetry suggests that the punishment of Cresseid should be left to Time and Change (Saturn and the Moon); this is approved. The parts of Cresseid affected by the sentence are precisely those by which most obviously she is related to Jupiter—her golden hair, her crystal eyes, and her clear voice.

One last point should be added. I have already noted passages which suggest that Cresseid knew she had become a leper when she returned to Calchas's house. It is certainly only after the sentence passed by the Gods that Henryson explicitly states this. Nevertheless, it would be mistaken to put these two events into direct temporal sequence, or a direct relationship of cause and effect. The process allegorized by the assembly of the gods is one which in realistic terms would occupy a considerable length of time. Henryson meant his audience, I believe, to realize this, to have noticed the earlier suggestions of physical change in Cresseid, and only to give them full significance after the dream allegory, the main function of which is to give them that full significance. The time sequence of medieval allegory seldom corresponds precisely to external reality, and in the *Testament* the dream-vision allegorizes Cresseid's behaviour from her desertion of Troilus to the full physical realization of the ultimate consequences.

6

Because her function is allegorical on one level only, Eurydice in *Orpheus and Eurydice* can possess no complexity of character. The *Testament* is less allegorical, but so far almost the same might be said of the character of Cresseid.

The parallels which have been indicated might even lead one
to think that in the *Testament* the equivalent of Orpheus is
Troilus. This is not so for a number of reasons. I have already
emphasized that Cresseid's offence against the physical laws
of the universe is one for which punishment is certain and final.
At the conclusion of the dream-vision the penalty has been
exacted: under that aspect, nothing more is possible except
the death of Cresseid. Calchas is the first to realize this:

> For he knew weill that thair was na succour
> To hir seiknes.
>
> (376–7)

Cresseid's leprosy, however, is a punishment for her violation
of the moral as well as the physical law, and here the last word
need not be punishment. Regeneration remains a possibility—
in *Orpheus and Eurydice* a possibility recognized by Orpheus's
almost successful attempt to rescue Eurydice from hell, an
attempt which was only feasible after the music of Orpheus
had been brought into accordance with the music of the
spheres. Thus in the *Testament* Troilus, who has no part in the
assembly of the planets, and who makes no attempt to rescue
Cresseid, does not play the part of Orpheus; his role is nearer
to that of Aristaeus. In the first part of the poem it is helpful to
regard Cresseid as the equivalent of Eurydice, but her function becomes more complex, combining in the latter part of
the poem allegorical features of Orpheus with those of
Eurydice. In *Orpheus and Eurydice* the planets teach Orpheus
to bring his music into some conformity with universal
harmony. Much the same is true of the sentence which they
pass on Cresseid, and in the second part of the *Testament*
Cresseid is to some extent her own Orpheus.

The process has a very partial and tentative beginning. Even when Cresseid seems to acknowledge her fault, her words still insinuate a condemnation of the gods who have punished her:

> Weiping full sair, 'Lo quhat it is' (quod sche),
> 'With fraward langage for to mufe and steir
> Our craibit Goddis, and sa is sene on me!
> My blaspheming now have I bocht full deir.'
>
> (351–4)

Craibit cancels whatever is conceded by *blaspheming*. In context, Calchas's message, delivered by a Chyld and intended to bring comfort, becomes bitingly ironical:

> The goddis wait all your Intent full weill.
>
> (364)

Cresseid's subsequent complaint in the leper-house (the third non-narrative interlude) follows her vision of the gods, but to some extent resembles that of Orpheus *before* he ascends to the spheres. The stanzaic form is similar; the *ubi sunt* motive is present in both; in both the emphasis is on loss:

> Thy greit triumphand fame and hie honour,
> Quhair thou was callit of Eirdlye wichtis Flour,
> All is decayit, thy weird is welterit so.
> Thy hie estait is turnit in darknes dour.
> This Lipper Ludge tak for thy burelie Bour.
> And for thy Bed tak now ane bunche of stro.
>
> (434–9)

Compare

> Fair weill my place, fair weill plesandis and play,
> And wylcum woddis wyld and wilsum way,
> My wicket werd in wildirness to ware;
> My rob ryell, and all my riche array,
> Changit salbe in rude russet and gray,

My dyademe in till a hate of hair;
My bed salbe with bever, brok, and bair,
In buskis bene with mony busteouss bess,
Withowttin song, sayand with siching sair,
'Quhair art thow gone, my luve Euridicess?'

(154–63)

The complaint of Orpheus was completely unsuccessful;
so on a first reading might appear the complaint of Cresseid.
But this is only superficial. Cresseid, for instance, has begun
to grasp the concept of Fortune, a concept only reached by
Orpheus when he has entered the underworld and seen
Ixion's wheel. Cresseid, it is true, begins merely from cruelty,
specifically as directed to herself—

Fell is thy Fortoun, wickit is thy weird.

(412)

Before the end of the complaint, however, she has put Fortune
into a perspective, more universal, although still biased:

O Ladyis fair of Troy and Grece, attend
My miserie, quhilk nane may comprehend,
My frivoll Fortoun, my Infelicitie,
My greit mischeif quhilk na man can amend.
Be war in tyme, approchis neir the end,
And in your mynd ane mirrour mak of me:
As I am now, peradventure that ye
For all your micht may cum to that same end,
Or ellis war, gif ony war may be . . .

Exempill mak of me in your Memour,
Quhilk of sic thingis wofull witnes beiris,
All Welth in Eird, away as Wind it weiris.
Be war thairfoir, approchis neir the hour:
Fortoun is fikkill, quhen scho beginnis & steiris.

(452–60, 465–9)

In these stanzas Cresseid's leprosy has become the type of all
inevitable suffering passively endured by humanity, a significance which gains in poignancy from the words of the Lipper
Lady which follow:

> I counsall the mak vertew of ane neid,
> To leir to clap thy Clapper to and fro,
> And leir efter the Law of Lipper Leid.
> (478–80)

At this stage of the poem the Law of Lipper Leid is Henryson's
general image for the human situation, of which Cresseid is
the particular example. The image gains force from the ig-
nobleness and general self-evident transience of the objects
to which Cresseid bids farewell:

> Quhair is thy Chalmer wantounlie besene? . . .
> The sweit Meitis, servit in plaittis clene,
> With Saipheron sals of ane gud sessoun:
> Thy gay garmentis with mony gudely Goun.
> (416, 420–2)

It is characteristic of the appetitive Cresseid of the first part
of the poem that she should dwell with such affection on
clothes, and the cleanliness of the plates from which she had
eaten sweetmeats: 'wantounlie' carries its own condemnation.
It is a sign of her more Orpheus-like qualities that even by the
end of the same complaint Cresseid should have realized the
inadequacy of her images.

The seeds of a further transition are perhaps to be seen in
the dominant metaphor of the complaint—the figure of gardens and particularly flowers, which has already been mentioned, and which indeed recurs thematically throughout the
poem. The image develops in three stages. Stanza 61 is a

farewell to the May landscape of the *Romance of the Rose* with its pretence of perpetual spring. Even the syntax of the verse—question, not statement—exposes the hollowness of the pretence, as indeed does the entire imagery. 'Greissis gay', 'fresche flowris', 'May', 'dew' are all traditional metaphors of transience: Flora, as queen of the defeated party of Idleness (the portress of the Garden of Deduit in the *Romance of the Rose*) is opposed to the victorious Diana in *The Flower and the Leaf*:[1] the Merle and Mawis are probably to be compared to the Merle, whose refrain 'A lusty lyfe in luves service bene' is opposed by Dunbar[2] to the Nightingale's 'All Luve is lost bot upone God allone'. The imagery expresses what Cresseid herself has not yet fully recognized, both the false standards which hitherto she has accepted, and the inevitability of the change which has overtaken her. The imagery too belongs to the stylistic tradition of the poetry of courtly love, and as I have already remarked, here, as perhaps always in Henryson's writings, the use of this courtly style implies a failure, a worldliness of moral judgement, on the part of the person who uses it, or who is so described.

This at first is not perceived by Cresseid, but the following stanza contains the beginning of realization, still on the limited, personal level:

> Thy greit triumphand fame and hie honour,
> Quhair thou was callit of Eirdlye wichtis Flour,
> All is decayit.

> (434–6)

---

[1] Ed. D. A. Pearsall (London and Edinburgh, 1962).

[2] 'The Merle and the Nightingale'; W. Mackay Mackenzie (ed.) *The Poems of William Dunbar* (London, 1932), pp. 134–7.

'Flour', especially in the context of 'Eirdlye wichtis' (a phrase surely which smacks of mortality), by effectively deflating the rhetorical pretence of 'greit triumphand fame and hie honour', opens the way for 'All is decayit' and the later cosmic images of fate and darkness. But these are still applied on the individual level, latterly even with some effect of deliberate anticlimax:

> This Lipper Ludge tak for thy burelie Bour.
> And for thy Bed tak now ane bunche of stro,
> For waillit Wyne, and Meitis thou had tho,
> Tak mowlit Breid, Peirrie and Ceder sour:
> Bot Cop and Clapper, now is all ago.
>
> (438–42)

Even now the appetitive reveals itself, as once again Cresseid remembers the food she had eaten in her 'triumphand' past.

The diction of stanzas 64 and 65, in which the flower image occurs for the third time, deserves some comment. These stanzas form an *envoi* addressed to the ladies of Troy and Greece, and show Cresseid attaining to universality, at least in so far as she sees her own fortune as typical of that of all beautiful women. Nevertheless, the universality suggested by the diction is greater still, and approaches that usually reserved for verse written in the tradition of the Falls of Princes. This is partly obtained by the imagery of Fortune, to which I have already referred, but it is strengthened by individual words, which in themselves either are not particularly appropriate to the 'Ladyis fair of Troy and Grece', or alternatively have in that context some appropriateness, but in the other a greater. Thus

> As I am now, peradventure that ye
> For all your micht may cum to that same end,
> Or ellis war, gif ony war may be.
>
> (458–60)

'Micht' surely belongs to the tradition of the Falls of Princes, as does

> Nocht is your famous laud and hie honour
> Bot wind Inflat in uther mennis eiris.
>
> (462–3)

or

> All Welth in Eird, away as Wind it weiris.
>
> (467)

Cresseid in fact herself consciously reaches a certain level of generality, but the diction in which she expresses it suggests a higher level still. This diction cannot but influence the third flower image, 'Nocht is your fairnes bot ane faiding flour', and make its application to all humanity—the level at which operates the character of Beauty in *Everyman*.

In the complaint, it should be added, we have thus three flower images, the first of flowers in spring, the second high summer, and the third autumn.

7

In the chapter on *Orpheus and Eurydice* I have already emphasized that Orpheus by himself is incapable of redeeming Eurydice from hell. When Cresseid has recognized the inevitability of her fall, and no longer kicks against the pricks, she has travelled as far on the path of redemption as intellect by itself is able. The conclusion of the *Testament* is one of the

most moving things in literature: perhaps as a consequence
it is extremely difficult to form a judgement on the precise
moral position which Cresseid reaches by the end—in
particular, whether in any sense she wins moral redemption.
Physically it is obvious that she cannot and does not, but I
have already drawn the distinction between physical and moral
redemption. Once again the parallel of *Orpheus and Eurydice*
is valuable. Eurydice was captured by hell when she fled from
Aristaeus and trod on the serpent. For Cresseid the corresponding step was her desertion of Troilus for Diomede,
and everything which that entailed. Diomede in the *Testament*
thus corresponds not to Aristaeus, but to the serpent, and as
I have already suggested Troilus should be regarded as the
equivalent of Aristaeus. This identification is already to be
found in Chaucer: indeed, there it is made by Criseyde herself when she is about to leave Troy. The reference is presu-
mably to Troilus as he appeared to Criseyde when he returned
from battle (II. 610–65), a scene which Henryson ironically
parallels in his final meeting of Troilus with Cresseid:

> For trusteth wel, that youre estat roial,
> Ne veyn delit, nor only worthinesse
> Of yow in werre or torney marcial,
> Ne pompe, array, nobleye, or ek richesse
> Ne made me to rewe on youre destresse;
> But moral vertue, grounded upon trouthe,
> That was the cause I first hadde on yow routhe!
>
> (IV. 1667–73)

The life of Troilus and Cresseid in Troy should thus be regarded as the period during which the operative habit of
moral virtue (Troilus) operated on the appetitive power of

the soul (Cresseid). Aristaeus, in other words, succeeded in ravishing Eurydice, who afterwards fell away from his government. In *Orpheus and Eurydice* Orpheus failed to rescue Eurydice from hell, because Aristaeus had disappeared after the failure of his attempt to ravish Eurydice. The background of the *Testament* is thus different from that of the *Orpheus and Eurydice*, and it differs still further in that at the conclusion of the poem Troilus reappears, and by his act of disinterested charity reasserts to the full the power of moral virtue which Cresseid had previously discarded. The effect is to make Cresseid realize not merely that her fate was inevitable, and therefore something to be shrugged off on to the shoulders of Fortune and the Gods, but that she herself held some, indeed the prime, responsibility. Her refrain contrasts 'fals Cresseid and trew Knicht Troylus', and the words which conclude this fourth non-narrative interlude, 'Nane but my self as now I will accuse', mark the moment of moral regeneration. It may be important, as E. M. W. Tillyard has suggested,[1] that she bequeaths her spirit to Diana, the victorious opponent of Flora in *The Flower and the Leaf*.

> My Spreit I leif to Diane quhair scho dwellis,
> To walk with hir in waist Woddis and Wellis.
>
> (587–8)

The conclusion of the poem is thus linked to, and incidentally transcends, the first movement of intellect experienced by Cresseid in the leper-house. The flower image makes its last appearance in the inscription on Cresseid's tomb—again in a context of 'fair Ladyis':

[1] Op. cit., pp. 17–18. But contrast Spearing, op. cit., p. 144, and D. Duncan, 'Henryson's *Testament of Cresseid*', *Essays in Criticism*, XI. 2 (1961), 128–35.

> Lo, fair Ladyis, Crisseid, of Troyis toun,
> Sumtyme countit the flour of Womanheid,
> Under this stane lait Lipper lyis deid.
>   (607–9)

It should be noticed that Henryson's presentation of the mutual failure of Troilus and Cresseid to recognize each other, is not merely realistic. On that level leprosy will account for both failures—Cresseid physically is so changed that Troilus does not know her, and the words in which she is described,

> Than upon him scho kest up baith hir Ene—
>   (498)

show that, as Cynthia had predicted, leprosy had affected her eyesight—that Cresseid was half-blind. Henryson is careful to use Aristotelian psychology to explain why Troilus should be reminded of Cresseid, even when he does not recognize her—again a realistic feature. But leprosy has already acquired an allegorical force in the poem; it is the visual representation of Cresseid's invisible sin. In this passage the allegory still holds—Virtue cannot recognize the appetite deformed by sin, though he may be stirred by it to the remembrance of unfallen appetite, and thus to an act of charity. Equally, appetite, deformed by sin, cannot recognize Virtue, except through an act of charity, which in effect symbolizes divine grace. This allegory is undoubtedly present, and I cannot see that the pathos of Henryson's realism is in any way diminished by its presence.

One last point. I have already emphasized the use made by Henryson of the diction of courtly love poetry, and in particular of the stylized descriptions of gardens in May. This, of course, is only one aspect of the poetry of courtly love, and the use Henryson makes of other aspects is quite different. Traditionally the relationship of lover and beloved was not evil, not even morally neutral, but positively good. As I have indicated, Henryson makes implicit use of this in his treatment of the original relationship between Troilus and Cresseid. But he does not leave it merely implicit. Cresseid in her final lament explicitly draws the contrast between her own behaviour in relationship to the code of courtly love, and that of Troilus:

> For lufe of me thou keipt gude continence,
> Honest and chaist in conversatioun.
> Of all wemen protectour and defence
> Thou was, and helpit thair opinioun.
> My mynd in fleschelie foull affectioun
> Was Inclynit to Lustis Lecherous:
> Fy fals Cresseid, O trew Knicht Troylus.
>
> (554–60)

On one level this belongs to the convention of the Religion of Love. In *The Romance of the Rose* the God of Love commands the lover

> For nothyng eke thy tunge applye
> To speke wordis of rebaudrye.
> To vilayn speche in no degre
> Lat never thi lippe unbounden be.
> For I nought holde hym, in good feith,
> Curteys, that foule wordis seith.
> And alle wymmen serve and preise,
> And to thy power her honour reise;
> And if that ony myssaiere
> Dispise wymmen, that thou maist here,
> Blame hym, and bidde hym holde hym stille.
>
> (2223–33)

In the *Troilus* Chaucer counterpointed Christianity and the religion of love, with Christianity only becoming dominant at the end, but then utterly overwhelming the religion of love. Henryson's method is different. There is no counterpoint, indeed there is no direct Christian reference whatsoever. In compensation, Henryson treats the courtly love relationship, and the religion of love, as types or allegories of relationships which in themselves are seen and judged in terms of Christian morality. It is a sign of the artistic independence which he finally reached that in this alone of his longer poems, he was content to leave the allegory to speak for itself; there is no *Moralitas*, as there is in the *Fabillis*, the *Orpheus and Eurydice*, and even, one might add, in *Troilus and Criseyde*.

IV

THE *MORALL FABILLIS*

Not in Fancy's Maze he wandered long,
But stoop'd to Truth and moralized his song.
POPE, *Epistle to Dr. Arbuthnot*

(*a*) INTRODUCTION

T HE reader who turns from the *Orpheus and Eurydice* or the *Testament of Cresseid* to the *Morall Fabillis of Esope the Phrygian* is at once aware of a difference akin in some ways to that which separates the earlier from the later poems of Pope. Partly at least the difference is one of stylistic level, which in the first two poems is usually high middle to high, in the last low to low middle. When high style does appear in the *Morall Fabillis*, it is introduced not for elevation, but usually for the sake of mock-heroic effect. One is aware too that in the *Morall Fabillis* Henryson includes much satirical contemporary reference, some of which is still recognizable, although the relevance of much of it has no doubt been completely lost. The Henryson of the *Morall Fabillis*, unlike the author of the other poems, is a satirist, whose effects are often something more than comic, although comedy is seldom long absent from his tales. It is in the *Morall Fabillis* that the reader most readily senses the poet who was also a lawyer and may well have had a fairly wide knowledge of the Europe of his day. For such a purpose the appropriate stylistic garb was the low or low middle; in the *Fabillis* as elsewhere Henryson keeps to the recognized stylistic criteria of his time.

Personal circumstances and personal inclinations probably had something to do with Henryson's adoption of a different mode, but the development of his work is not to be explained simply in such terms. In his other major narratives Henryson was working from models which he regarded as primarily elevated—Boethius' *De Consolatione* and Chaucer's *Troilus and Criseyde*. In the *Fabillis* his sources belong to a different literary *genre*: he made use for instance of the *Roman de Renart*,[1] which might be taken as the very type of non-courtly medieval poetry. The Æsopic fable too has an interesting position in the literary thought of the day, as may most easily be shown from a work to which Henryson's debt has already been shown, Boccaccio's *De Genealogia Deorum*. Boccaccio's last two books form an interesting defence of poetry in terms of the assumed presence of allegory in all worthwhile poems. For Boccaccio, that is to say, all poetry is in some sense fable —indeed *fabula* is the word normally used by him to mean 'narrative poem'. I shall discuss some aspects of his doctrine at greater length below; for the present it is sufficient to note that he made[2] a fourfold classification of the *fabula*. His first type was the Æsopic, his second the epic, or Virgilian, his third the fable of transformation, which might be called the Ovidian. The fourth need not enter the discussion; Boccaccio

---

[1] See the appendixes for sources and for the text used in quotations from the *Morall Fabillis*. I have expanded abbreviations, normalized the use of *þ*, *u*, *v* and *w*, *i*, and *j*, and have begun lines with capitals in texts based on Bannatyne.

[2] XIV. ix.

felt that some room had to be made for narratives in which he could find no allegorical content, and which accordingly he regarded as worthless. It is the dignity of the company kept by Æsop in Boccaccio which must be emphasized; he ranks with Virgil and Ovid, although it is clear that Boccaccio regarded him as belonging properly to a rather lower level— a level which would be accompanied by a corresponding lowering of style, but not necessarily of intellectual content. Henryson's immediate Æsopic models were probably the Latin verse-*Romulus* of Gualterus Anglicus, and its derivative, the French *Isopet de Lyon*[1]—and it is worth noting that in both the normal level of style is low middle or low. In his other poems Henryson may be regarded as writing Virgilian fables; in the *Morall Fabillis* he turned from Virgilian to Æsopic, with all that the transfer necessarily implied.

Henryson imitated the verse-*Romulus* and the *Isopet de Lyon* in providing his *Fabillis* with a general Prologue, but he wrote more consciously in a tradition of literary theory and criticism than did the authors of either of his models. It is in fact in Boccaccio that the closest parallels are to be found, although the germ of the theory is already to be found in a celebrated couplet from the *Ars Poetica* of Horace—

> Aut prodesse volunt aut delectare poetae;
> Aut simul et iucunda et idonea dicere vitae—
>
> (333-4)

Horace's doctrine was much developed in later antiquity, as for instance in the *Super Thebaiden*, a commentary on the *Thebaid* of Statius attributed to Fulgentius.[2] In Fulgentius

---

[1] See Appendix II.   [2] Ed. R. Helm (Teubner, 1898), pp. 180–6.

is to be found the commonplace of the kernel and shell of the
nut, adapted by Henryson—'testa insipida est, nucleus sapo-
rem gustandi reddit: similiter non littera, sed figura palato
intelligentiae sapit'.[1] Boccaccio in turn developed the argument further. To a greater extent than Fulgentius, Boccaccio
emphasizes that the pleasure derived from fictitious narrative
is wholesome and recreative: in Henryson one may compare

> As clerkis sayis, it is rycht proffitable
> Amang ernyst to myng a mirry sport,
> To blyth the spreit, and gar the tyme be schort.
>
> (19–21)

To a greater extent, too, he emphasizes the 'subtlety' of the
allegory as promoting the ultimate 'sweetness' of poetry.
'Subtilitas'—which is often to be equated with 'obscurity'—
is a recurring term in his critical vocabulary.[2] One notes the
parallel of Henryson's 'scitell dyt of poetre', and the emphasis
—'so it be lawborit with grit diligence'—which is laid on
effort in the understanding of poetry.

Boccaccio's general account is to be found in Book XIV,
where his chapter headings may indicate some of the ways in
which his literary doctrine is connected to that of Henryson.
IX, for instance, has 'Composuisse fabulas apparet utile
potius quam damnosum'; X, 'Stultum credere poetas nil
sensisse sub cortice fabularum'; and XII, 'Damnanda non est
obscuritas poetarum'. It is in Chapter IX that Boccaccio
discusses the meaning of the word *fabula*, which he defines
scholastically thus: 'Fabula est exemplaris seu demonstrativa
sub figmento locutio, cuius amoto cortice, patet intentio

---

[1] Ibid., p. 180.
[2] Compare especially J. W. H. Atkins, *English Literary Criticism: The
Medieval Phase* (London, 1952), pp. 163–81.

fabulantis.' Of the general term he makes the fourfold sub-
division already mentioned, the first of which is characterized
by a completely unrealistic convention of assuming that
animals and even inanimate objects have the ability to speak
('animalia bruta aut etiam insensata inter se loquentia induci-
mus'). In phraseology that recalls Henryson's, he takes Æsop
as the type of the narrative poet whose work belongs to this
category: 'Et autor harum permaximus fuit Esopus, vir Gre-
cus antiquitate ac etiam gravitate venerabilis.' Like Henryson,
Boccaccio emphasizes the universal appeal of the fables: 'Et
dato his non solum civile vulgus, sed etiam agrestes utantur,
ut plurimum, non fastidivit aliquando suis libris inserere
Aristotiles, celestis ingenii vir et Perypatheticorum princeps
phylosophorum.'

The importance of the Prologue, however, is not limited
to the partial exposition of a Boccaccian theory of narrative
poetry; Henryson's practical observations are equally important. He conventionally disclaims skill in rhetoric.

> In hamely langage and in termes rud
> Me neidis wryt, for quhy of eloquence
> No rethory I nevir undirstud.
> Thairfoir meikly I pray your reverens,
> Gife ye fynd ocht that throw my negligence
> Be diminut, or yit superfluys,
> Correct it at your willis gracius.
>
> (36–42)

Such disclaimers are usually the sign of a thorough training in
the rhetorical curriculum; the 'modesty formula' has a long
history in literature. Even a stylist so refined as Tacitus would
have us believe that his Agricola was composed 'in artless

and unschooled language'.[1] Tacitus' purpose, like that of
others, was to win his readers' favour by a display of diffidence
at the beginning of a literary work—a process recommended,
for instance, by the anonymous author of the influential *Ad
Herennium*.[2] But in addition to this, the terms used by Henryson indicate with some precision the stylistic level to which he
aspired. He aimed at a language normally neither 'diminut'
nor 'superfluys'—almost certainly an indication that he aimed,
not at a technically low style, which for his purposes would
be 'diminut', nor at a 'superfluys' high style (one should perhaps think of some of Lydgate's work), but at a mean—some
form of the middle style. So far as one can judge over a gap
of some five hundred years, the general stylistic level of the
Fabillis would support this reading, although it must be
assumed that when occasion demanded Henryson allowed his
style to modulate into high or low, or even a burlesque of high
—the mock-heroic.

For the rest, Henryson divides his Prologue into two sec-
tions, in the first of which he makes his general defence of the
narrative form. All narrative poetry is allegorical and therefore fable. Henryson supports his argument by three metaphors and one proverb. The metaphors are adapted to his
doctrine. That of the cultivated earth suggests the life-giving
quality of poetry. That of nut and kernel suggests both the
sweetness and the difficulty of poetry. That of the bow
exemplifies the proverb which precedes it, and simultaneously
amplifies it in terms of sport and war. All three metaphors have

[1] E. R. Curtius, op. cit., p. 83.
[2] I. v. 8. I have used H. Caplan's edition in the Loeb Classical Library
(1954).

a proverbial quality which Henryson would have regarded
as heightening the persuasiveness of style and argument.

The second part of the Prologue is directly concerned with
Æsop's Fables. Much of it has already been discussed; the
most notable feature of the remainder is the emphasis laid on
'carnall fowll delyte' (51), in terms of which the Æsopic
equation of man with beast is appropriate. As much as in the
Orpheus and Eurydice or the *Testament of Cresseid*, Henryson's concern is with the carnal passions of fallen man. Eurydice and Cresseid both represent appetite and the appetitive;
the emphasis in the *Fabillis* is nowhere very different—'he in
brutall beist be transformat' (56).

One last point. Henryson claims that 'a morall sueit sentence' springs out of the 'scitell dyt of poetre'. Some kind of
Moralitas, that is to say, is always to be found in poetry.
Henryson does not claim, nor do his own *Moralitates* indicate, that in poetry every detail must have an allegorical meaning. Nor does he imply that a single *sentence* only is to be
found in a poem. Fully detailed allegory occurs in some of the
fables, in others the *sentence* may derive from one of several
narrative incidents. Sometimes too the narrative detail will
suggest one form of *sentence*, which, however, Henryson
avoids in his *Moralitas*, while concentrating on a particular
interpretation of a single episode.

(*b*) *The Cock and the Jasp*
(*The Taill of the Cok, and the Jasp*)

The Cock and the Jasp, which is so closely linked to the *Prologue*, exemplifies the doctrines of the *Prologue* more literally
and in more strikingly Biblical terms than any other of the

fables.[1] It is obvious, for instance, that the *Moralitas* has Biblical overtones. Less obvious is the precision with which these overtones are used. They refer primarily to the Wisdom literature of the Old Testament and Apocrypha, particularly to Proverbs. Henryson identifies 'science' of the *Moralitas* with Biblical Wisdom; by his choice of diction he draws an implied ironic parallelism between the prudent 'digging out' Wisdom, and the cock scraping the jasp out of the dunghill. Compare Proverbs ii. 3–6:

'Si enim sapientiam invocaveris, et inclinaveris cor tuum prudentiae;

Si quaesieris eam quasi pecuniam, et sicut thesauros effoderis illam;

Tunc intelliges timorem Domini, et scientiam Dei invenies, Quia Dominus dat sapientiam, et ex ore ejus prudentia et scientia.'

With these verses, and Proverbs viii. 12,

'Ego sapientia, habito in consilio; et eruditis intersum cogitationibus.'

compare also in Henryson

> This gentill Jesp, oft different in hew,
> Betakinis perfyt *prudens* and *cunnyng*.   (127–8)

With 'moir excelland than ony erdly thing' (130) compare Proverbs viii. 11:

'Melior est enim sapientia cunctis pretiosissimis; et omne desiderabile ei non potest comparari.'

---

[1] Compare D. Fox, 'Henryson's *Fables*', *E.L.H.* xxix (1962), pp. 337–56. Professor Fox's article also deals with *The Preaching of the Swallow*.

or alternatively Proverbs iii. 15:

'Pretiosior est cunctis opibus; et omnia quae desiderantur huic non valent comparari.'

Proverbs viii. 15–16 is the most probable source of 'Quha can govern citie and burchgus?' (136):

'Per me reges regnant, et legum conditores justa decernunt. Per me principes imperant, et potentes decernunt justitiam.'

Job xxviii. 13, 'Nescit homo pretium ejus', provides the nearest parallel to 'That may nocht with no erdly thing be bocht' (151).

In the *Moralitas* the jasp is opposed to the cock as in Proverbs Wisdom is opposed to the Fool.

> This cok, desyring moir the symple corne
> Thane only Jasp, Onto the fule is peir,
> Makand at science bot a knak and skorne.
>
> (141–3)

Compare Proverbs i. 7 and *passim*:

'Timor Domini principium sapientiae. Sapientiam atque doctrinam stulti despiciunt.'

The resemblance between the *Moralitas* and the Wisdom literature is thus striking enough, but at the same time it remains somewhat unspecific—the resemblance is general rather than particular. This brings out the more strikingly two passages which have a very specific reference. The first of these is 138–9:

> It is the riches that evir sall indure,
> Quhilk motht, nor must may nother rust nor ket.

The reference here is to the New Testament—Matthew vi. 19–20—part of the Sermon on the Mount:

'Nolite thesaurizare vobis thesauros in terra, ubi aerugo et tinea demolitur, et ubi fures effodiunt, et furantur.

Thesaurizate autem vobis thesauros in caelo, ubi neque aerugo, neque tinea demolitur, et ubi fures non effodiunt, nec furantur.'

(The link between *effodiunt* in these verses, *effoderis* in Proverbs ii. 4, quoted above, and the basic metaphor of the fable should not be missed. This verse equates the cock with the man who laid up treasures on earth, or alternatively with the thieves.)

The other reference is also to a passage from the Sermon on the Mount, Matthew vii. 6. With Henryson's

> His hairt wamillis gud argumentis till heir,
> As dois the sow, to quhome men for the nons,
> In hir drafe troch wald saw the pretius stons.

compare
$(145–7)$

'Nolite dare sanctum canibus, neque mittatis margaritas vestras ante porcos, ne forte conculcent eas pedibus suis, et conversi dirumpant vos.'

Each of these in turn leads inevitably to the various parables of the Kingdom, in which treasure or jewellery appears, in particular to Matthew xiii. 44–46:

'Simile est regnum caelorum thesauro abscondito in agro; quem qui invenit homo, abscondit, et prae gaudio illius vadit, et vendit universa quae habet, et emit agrum illum.

Iterum simile est regnum caelorum homini negotiatori, quaerenti bonas margaritas.

Inventa autem una pretiosa margarita, abiit, et vendidit omnia quae habuit, et emit eam.'

With 'thesauro abscondito' in particular may be compared
'hid' in

> Bot now, allaiss, this Jasp is tynt and hyd
>
> (155)

as may also Matthew xiii. 33:

'Simile est regnum caelorum fermento, quod acceptum
mulier abscondit in farinae satis tribus, donec fermentatum
est totum.'

'Tynt', on the other hand, is probably to be compared with
Luke xv. 8:

'Aut quae mulier habens drachmas decem, si perdiderit
drachmam unam, nonne accendit lucernam, et everrit domum,
et quaerit diligenter, donec inveniat?'

A further point to link the language of the *Moralitas* to the
New Testament is perhaps the similarity of 'vendit universa
quae habet' and 'vendidit omnia quae habuit' to

> Weill war the man of all uthir, that mocht
> All his lyfe dayis in perfyte study war
> To get science; for him neidit no mair.
>
> (152–4)

The final New Testament element is the Johannine, based
on Revelation as well as the Fourth Gospel. Henryson probably calls the jewel a jasp because in Revelation xxi. 10–11
the New Jerusalem, the City of God, is described as a jasp:

'Et sustulit me in spiritu in montem magnum et altum, et
ostendit mihi civitatem, sanctam Jerusalem, descendentem
de caelo a Deo,

Habentem claritatem Dei, et lumen ejus simile lapidi pre-
tioso, tanquam lapidi jaspidis, sicut crystallum.'

The other Johannine reference is to John vi. 27. Henryson's

> And to manis saull it is eternall met
>
> (140)

clearly refers to

'Operamini non cibum qui perit, sed qui permanet in vitam aeternam.'

The *Moralitas* thus expounds the *Taill* in terms of Old Testament Wisdom and New Testament Kingdom and City. In the *Taill* itself, such references for the most part are absent. The *Moralitas* may lead one to see a double significance in the phrase 'Screpand amang the ass' (68), or to compare

> I had levir go skraip heir with my nailis,
> Among this moll, and luk my lyvis fude,
> As corne, or drafe, small wormis, or snaillis,
> Or ony meit wald do my stomok gude,
> Nor of Jespis a mekle multitude.   (92–96)

with the injunction quoted above not to cast pearls before swine, 'ne forte conculcent eas pedibus suis'. The word 'drafe' too gains additional significance from its use in the *Moralitas*. In all these, however, *Taill* depends on *Moralitas*; so far as I have been able to observe, only stanza 11 by itself demands a definite Biblical reference:

> As madynis wantoun and insolent,
> That fane wald play, and on the streit be sene,
> To swopyne of the houss takis no tent,
> Quhat be thairin, swa that the flure be clene;
> Jowalis ar tint, as oft tymes hes bene sene,
> And in the swoupyne is castin furth annone—
> Peraventour, swa wass the samyn stone.
>
> (71–77)

The primary reference here is to a parable already mentioned, that of the Lost Silver (Luke xv. 8):

'Aut quae mulier habens drachmas decem, si perdiderit drachmam unam, nonne accendit lucernam, et everrit domum, et quaerit diligenter, donec inveniat.' Sweeping, it is assumed in the parable, is a carefully conducted operation, which leads to the discovery of lost treasure. Henryson's 'madynis' act in the opposite way. In the *Moralitas*, that is to say, the scriptural references harmonize with the literal meaning; in the *Taill* the two are opposed, and the maidens contrasted with Luke's *mulier* in a way suggested, perhaps, by Luke xi. 24–25:

'Cum immundus spiritus exierit de homine, ambulat per loca inaquosa, quaerens requiem, et non inveniens, dicit: Revertar in domum meam unde exivi.

Et cum venerit, invenit eam scopis mundatam et ornatam.'

In the *Moralitas* the relation between overtones and literal meaning is harmonic; in the *Taill* it is contrapuntal.

This leads to a further observation. One may probably assume that Henryson and the audience for whom he wrote were prepared to accept Biblical authority as final. The Biblical references thus provide a norm by which the relative validity of point of view in *Taill* and *Moralitas* may be indicated. The fable as a whole consists of two balanced expositions of opposed points of view—the five stanzas in which the cock addresses the jasp, and the five in which the omniscient narrator states the *Moralitas*. (As narrative, the fable is negligible. There is no plot; the action consists of the stanza in which the cock finds the jasp, and the one in which he leaves it. The *raison d'être* of the fable is not to be found in these.)

The opposition between the two points of view is absolute, to a degree even surprisingly so. So long as one confines oneself to the cock, one's main impression may be of a comfortable and satisfying rationality, not unlike that of the *Moralitas* in *The Taill of the Uponlandis Mous, and the Burges Mouse:*

> Off erdly Joy it beiris most degre,
> Blythness in hairt, with small possessioun.
>
> (234–5)

The major difference might appear to be a deliberate reduction of level of diction from middle to low style:

> I lawfe fer bettir thing of less availl,
> As cafe, or corne, to fill my tome entrell.
>
> (90–91)

Three points must, however, be added. In the first place, the speaker is a cock on his own dunghill. The proverbial implication is obvious, and is exploited by Henryson here and elsewhere. In the first stanza he described the cock as

> Rycht cant and crouss, suppoiss he was bot pure.
>
> (65)

The cock, as in the *Moralitas* of *The Taill of Schir Chantecleir and the Foxe*, is a type of pride, in the present instance false intellectual pride. In the second place, even as he rejects it, the cock recognizes clearly the worth of the jasp; there is an extravagance in 'fer bettir' which emphasizes how violently he rejects something at the same time as he recognizes its true relative worth in the phrase 'thing of less availl'. Thirdly, the things that he loves far better are grossly physical—'ony meit wald do my stomok gude'. The 'cafe' is perhaps to be compared with the husks in the parable of the

Prodigal; certainly the word is most often used in connexion
with swine—compare the 'drafe troch' in the *Moralitas*. 'Small
wormis, or snaillis' in stanza 14 reduces the stylistic level still
further, and re-emphasizes the physical, which has now become even the repulsive, though it is still, I suppose, appropriate for a cock. The speech in fact satisfies because it is so
strictly animal.

Even here, however, Henryson does not employ only a low
style of the kind described. Half the effect of the passages I
have quoted comes from the stylistic contrast they present to
other lines in the same stanzas. For instance,

>   As cafe, or corne, to fill my tome entrell

is balanced against the Latin diction of

>   Thy grit vertew, nor yit thy cullour cleir,
>   I may nowther extoll nor magnify.
>
>   (86–87)

So

>   As corne, or drafe, small wormis, or snaillis

rises to the following line, which might perhaps be regarded
as middle style,

>   Or ony meit wald do my stomok gude,

which in turn rises to Latin diction and the high style:

>   Nor of Jespis a mekle multitude.

The cock's speech concludes with a stanza in high style,
which effectively uses the device of rhetorical question:

>   Quhair suld thow mak thy habitatioun?
>   Quhair suld thow dwell, bot in a ryall tour?
>   Quhair suld thow sit, bot one a kingis croun,

> Exalt in wirchep and in gret honour?
> Ryss, gentill Jaspis, of all stonis the flour,
> Out of this ass, and pass quhair thow suld be;
> Thow ganis nocht for me, nor I for the.
>
> (106–12)

Here too, however, there is a contrast, a contrast established by the single 'low' word, 'ass', and stressed by the moral and rhetorical anticlimax of the final line. Henryson completes the effect by deliberately balancing the stanza against stanza 20 in the *Moralitas*.

> Quha may be rycht hardy and gratious?
> Quha can eschew perrell and aventure?
> Quha can govern citie and burchgus
> Without science? non, I yow ensure.
> It is the riches that evir sall indure,
> Quhilk motht, nor must, may nother rust nor ket,
> And to manis saull it is eternall met.
>
> (134–40)

The rhetorical structure is parallel, and the stanza works towards a satisfactory moral and rhetorical climax.

I do not think that in this there is any ambiguity. The pleasure one takes in the passages of low style does not undercut the authority of the passages in high style, as even the cock recognizes. Clearly, the cock's action is wilful and foolish. Nevertheless, the speech by itself indicates no more than his wilfulness and foolishness; it does not show the precise terms in which these failings are to be judged. This is the function, primarily of the *Moralitas*, but also of the stanza which sets forth the seven properties of the jasp, and more particularly the contrapuntal Biblical overtones in stanza 2—overtones which are taken up and amplified in the *Moralitas*.

The style of the *Taill* as opposed to the *Moralitas* is characterized then by counterpoint of narrative against overtones,
and one level of diction against another. To this nothing in the
Moralitas corresponds. The level of diction is lowered in the
three lines which describe the cock in terms of Matthew vii. 6:

> His hairt wamillis gud argumentis till heir,
> As dois the sow, to quhome men for the nons,
> In hir drafe troch wald saw the pretius stons.
>
> (145–7)

Here 'wamillis', 'sow', and 'drafe troch' belong to a stylistic
level lower than that of the remainder of the *Moralitas* ('Sow',
it should be noted, is somewhat lower even than the scriptural
porcos). But there is no question of counterpoint—the style
is lowered to correspond to the lower subject-matter. In the
Taill the reader is apparently expected to accept material, the
expression of which is on a lower level than that which he is
expected to reject. In the *Moralitas* there is no such paradox.
The counterpoint of the *Taill* is resolved into the harmony of
the *Moralitas*, and the virtue of the poem as a whole is the
satisfactory resolution of the apparent conflict of the two.

(c) *The Frog and the Mouse*
(*The Taill of the Paddok and the Mous*)

Allegory in the Middle Ages was particularly, though not, of
course, exclusively, the concern of the Friars. Thus, for example, the Dominican, Thomas Aquinas, gave classical
expression to the theory of allegorical scriptural exegesis in
his *Summa Theologica* I. 10. On the practical side, the sermons
of the Friars came to centre more and more on *exempla*, 'the

exemplification of truth in a narrative'—a narrative which might afterwards be given allegorical interpretation on one or more of the levels discussed by Aquinas.[1] Throughout the *Fabillis*, Henryson in a sense wrote in this tradition; it is in the *Moralitas* of *The Taill of the Paddok and the Mous*, however, that the fact is explicitly, albeit ironically, recognized:

> Adew, my freind, and gife that ony speiris
> Of this fable so schortly I conclude,
> Thou say I left the laif unto the freiris
> To mak a sample or similitud.

(193–6)

'Sample' or the variant 'exempill' is a vernacular rendering of Latin *exemplum*. Henryson is saying that he has himself already treated the *Taill* as an *exemplum*, but that he has left room still for the Friars. The irony is directed, not so much at the allegoric method, as at the extremes of length and ingenuity to which the Friars sometimes carried it. Again, it was central to the allegoric method that an interpretation might be made at one or more of three spiritual levels. The *Moralitas* of *The Taill of the Paddok and the Mous* is unique in that it is divided, metrically and otherwise, into two parts, three eight-line ballade stanzas, and six stanzas of rhyme-royal. The first and less interesting of these contains moral advice on the danger of close association with a smooth-tongued hypocrite. This is interpretation on the first, or tropological level, which, as St. Bonaventura pointed out,[2] is particularly suitable for preachers. The second interprets the various features of the

[1] Compare especially G. R. Owst, *Literature and Pulpit in Medieval England* (2nd edit., Oxford, 1961), pp. 56 ff.

[2] *Opusculum de Reductione Artium ad Theologiam, Opera Omnia* (Ad Claras Aquas, 1891), v. 321.

story—the paddock as man's body, the mouse as his soul, the water as the world, the gled as death—on the level of allegory proper, the 'sence allegorik' which is found 'whan a man understondith bi a bodili thyng that he redith of in story an other gostli thyng that is betokened therbi',[1] and which, says Bonaventura, is particularly suitable for doctors. Perhaps deliberately, there is no interpretation on the level particularly suited to contemplatives, the third or anagogical, by which a narrative is understood as a figure of future glory. This may be the similitude which is left to the Friars, with a hint, perhaps, that they are all too ready to expound that state in detail. But there is at least an indication of the anagogical interpretation in the concluding triplet:

> Now Chryst for us that deit on the rud,
> Of saule and luf as thou art salviour,
> Grant us to pass in till a blissit hour.
>
> (1797–9)

Water, the central image in this second section of the *Moralitas*, is one of the most widespread and powerful symbols of the allegorical tradition, and one upon which the entire interpretation of the poem must be based. For Bede at the beginning of the allegoric tradition in Britain,[2] as for Henryson at the end,

> The waltir is the warld ay walterand
> With mony wayiss of tribulatioun.
>
> (179–80)

But many further associations which clustered about the image

---

[1] Owst, op. cit., p. 59, footnote 5. The quotation is from MS. Harl. 2276, fols. 32b–33.

[2] J. A. Giles (ed.), *Patres Ecclesiae Anglicanae* (London, 1843–44), x. 67.

are to be found in the *Fabill*. Boethius and others made water the emblem of the Goddess Fortuna, with her near-absolute control over human beings until the moment of death.[1] Variability was her characteristic, symbolized by the treacherous changes of the sea from calm to storm, and at other times by the image of the turning wheel. Human beings alone were affected by her; save for the little world of man, the entire universe gave evidence only of order. The complaint of Boethius is that 'Mankind is no base part of this great work, and we are tossed on Fortune's wave'.[2] It is from this point of view that the aquatic paddock or toad is so apt an image of the human body, absolutely subject to the power of Fortune, and it is in terms of a relationship to Fortune that the *significatio* of the paddock is presented. At the beginning the aquatic image is emphasized, but in the second stanza that of the wheel comes to predominate, and it is with this that the stanza ends:

> This paddok usand in this flud to dwell
> Is manis body, sumand air and lait
> Into this warld with cairis implicat,
> Now he now law, quhyle plungit up and doun,
> Ay in to perrell and redy for to droun:
>
> Now dolorus, now blyth as bird on breir,
> Now in fredome, now wardit in distress,
> Now haill, now sound, now deid and brocht on beir,
> Now pure as Job, now rowand in riches;
> Now gownis gay, now brattis to imbrass,

[1] II, Prosa 3, 48–50.
[2] I, Metrum 5, 44–45.
> Operis tanti pars non uilis
> Homines quatimur fortunae salo.

Now full as fysche, now hungry as a hound,
Now on the quheill, now wappit to the ground.
(160–71)

As may be seen in the quotation from Boethius, the individual in relation to the sea of Fortune is often symbolized by
a boat and its occupant at the mercy of the waves. This image
is not found in the *Moralitas*, but it is at least subliminally
present in the *Taill*. Thus, when the mouse explains her pre-
dicament to the paddock, she says

I haif no boit, heir is no mareneir,
And thocht thair ware, I haif no fraucht to pay.
(22–23)

The paddock promises

Do my counsall and I sall fynd the way,
Withouttin horss, brig, boit, or yit gallay,
To bring you our saifly, be nocht affeird,
And nocht to weit the campis of your beird.
(25–28)

She, it appears, is to play the part of a boat:

With my twa feit, quod scho, lukkin and braid,
In steid of airis I row the streme full still.
(36–37)

To play the part of a boat, however, is not to be a boat, and
the significance of the distinction is made plain by a passage
from the A-text of *Piers Plowman*,[1] the Prologue to the *Vita
de Do-Wel, Do-Bet and Do-Best*, a passage in which, significantly enough, a Friar expounds the text *Sepcies in die cadit
iustus* (based on Proverbs xxiv. 16):

[1] Ed. G. Kane (London, 1960). All references to the A-text are to this
edition.

þe watir is liknid to þe world þat waniþ & waxiþ;
þe goodis of þis ground be lik þe grete wawes,
þat as wyndis & watris walwen aboute;
þe boot is liknid to þe body þat britel is of kynde,
þat þoruȝ þe fend, & þe flessh, & þe false world,
Synnes þe sad man seuene siþes in þe day.
Ac dedly synne doþ he nouȝt, for dowel hym helpiþ,
þat is charite þe champioun, chief helpe aȝens synne.
For he strengþeþ þe to stonde & steriþ þi soule
þat, þeiȝ þi body bowe as bot doþ in þe watir,
Ay is þi soule sauf but þou þiself wilt
Folewe þi flesshis wil & þe fendis aftir,
And don dedly synne & drenche þiseluen.
God wile suffre þe to deiȝe so, for þiself hast þe maistrie.

(34–47)

The body, it is clear, only becomes a boat which carries the
soul safely across the world when the soul itself is justified, or
redeemed; in other words, when the body is the instrument,
rather than the master, or even partner, of the soul. Charity
is then the helmsman, the mariner whom the mouse cannot
find. The situation in the *Taill* is reversed; the soul follows the
body, which is therefore symbolized not by a boat, but by the
paddock, an animal which actively tries to drown the mouse.
All the imagery of the passage agrees in this. There is no
helmsman. The body offers to carry the soul to the other side

Withouttin horss, brig, boit, or yit gallay.

Boit and *Gallay* have perhaps the same significance; *Brig*
refers almost certainly to the work of the organized Church
(*pontifex*, 'bridge-maker', 'priest'), while the significance of
Hors is perhaps to be discovered in the usual patristic and
medieval exposition of the parable of the Good Samaritan

(Luke x. 30–35), according to which the Samaritan's beast symbolizes the Flesh, with Christ as the Samaritan.[1] Compare also Theodulph's *Gloria, Laus et honor*,[2] with its concluding couplet

> sis pius ascensor, tuus et nos simus asellus,
> tecum nos capiat urbs veneranda Dei.

(The connexion of this with the last three lines of the *Moralitas* is fairly obvious.) The central theme of the poem thus becomes the hopeless attempt of the individual soul to reach salvation without the assistance of Christ, Church, or conversion, an attempt which can only lead to disaster.

So far the sea aspect of the water image has been dominant. That is to take the mouse's (that is to say, the human) point of view, but that of course is to confine one's attention to a single part of the *Taill*. The poem begins from a more general point of view, not with a sea, but with a river, which might be waded by anyone not so small as a mouse, or which at least (and this gains point from the *significatio* of the *Hors* already discussed) is fordable on horseback:

> Upone a tyme, as Ysop can report,
> A littill mouss come till a rever syd.
> Scho mycht nocht waid, hir schankis were so schort:
> Scho couth nocht soume, scho had no horss till ryd.
>
> (1–4)

To the mouse, however, the river is a great expanse of water, described by her first as a 'bryme' (OE. *brim*, sea, water of sea, lake': cf. *brimliþend*, seafarer), and afterwards as 'this

---

[1] J. P. Migne, *Patrologia Latina*, 92, pp. 469–70.
[2] I have used the version in S. Gaselee (ed.) *The Oxford Book of Medieval Latin Verse* (Oxford, 1928), pp. 41–42.

wattir greit'. The mouse's point of view, in fact, is used to link two separate symbols, the sea, which subjectively is present to the mouse, and the river, which in terms of the poem is a fact. The river image, in turn, introduces another series of associations, which may most readily be illustrated from the tradition of the *Romance of the Rose*,[1] where the river passing the Garden of Deduit is the Water of Life, and thus the passage of Time, an image further developed, for instance, in *Pearl*,[2] where the dreamer is separated from his dead daughter by a river which cannot be crossed before death:

> þou wylyeȝ ouer þys water to weue;
> Er moste þou ceuer to oþer counsayle:
> þy corse in clot mot calder keue.
> For hit watȝ forgarte at Paradys greue.
>
> (318–21)

In this way the image merges with that of the sea of Fortune, from which man escapes only at death. In *Pearl*, however, the river is that which issues from the throne of God (Revelation xxii. 1), and beyond it lies the vision of peace, the New Jerusalem. The *Taill* includes a mouse's eye view of the same vision:

> Seis thou, quod scho, of corne yone Joly flat,
> Of ryp aitis, of beir, of peiss and quheit?
> I am hungry and fane wald be thairat,
> But I am stoppit heir be this wattir greit.
>
> (15–18)

a stanza which is duly explained in the *Moralitas*:

---

[1] Compare Lewis, *Allegory of Love*, p. 119.
[2] Ed. E. V. and Ida L. Gordon (Oxford, 1953).

> The natur of the saule wald our be borne
> Out of this warld unto the hevinly trone.
>
> (184–5)

Two points remain. Before death, soul and body have no separate temporal existence. It follows that the earthly life of man is symbolized only by the attempt to cross the stream —in other words by the four stanzas which begin

> Than fute for fute thay lap baith in the brime.
>
> (99)

Nothing else is to be interpreted in temporal terms. This is the distortion of time so characteristic of allegory. One might compare the *Romance of the Rose*,[1] where the slow progress of a courtly love affair from first meeting to the eventual recognition by the lady of the lover as worthy of some favour, is symbolized by the shooting of five arrows in quick succession. That the attempted crossing must be interpreted as man's life is shown by the *Moralitas*, where the ups and downs of the progress are interpreted in terms which postulate the passage of a considerable length of time:

> Now he, now law, quhyle plungit up and doun,
> Ay in to perrell and redy for to droun.
>
> (163–4)

in fact, from birth or conception ('Tuk threid and band her leg, as scho hir bad', 98) to death.

In the second place, the discussion on the bank is outside time, and should not thus be regarded as occupying time. It is the instantaneous opposition of soul to body at their joint conception. The soul is created at the same time as it is infused

---

[1] This occupies lines 1719–1926 of the Chaucerian version.

into the body. The soul must be united to the body, which is necessary to it for the operation of the sensitive part, while at the same time it is incorruptible, not subject, nor even necessarily relevant, to time[1] (see the discussion of *Orpheus and Eurydice* above). Since Adam's fall, the body has been corruptible, and as subject to time as to sin. This is the theological explanation of the mouse's outcry,

> Suld I be bund and fast quhair I am fre
> In howp of help?
>
> (85–86)

which might be paraphrased at a different stylistic level, 'Should I be infused into a body, and so made subject to time, when at the moment time has no authority over me, but I cannot otherwise obtain salvation'? One should compare the first words of the mouse in the *Taill*:

> 'Help our, help our,' the silly mowss can cry,
> 'For Godis lufe, sum body our this bryme.'
>
> (8–9)

The word 'body' is used in a quite literal sense. The mouse's wonder at the power of the paddock,

> 'I haif mervell,' than quod the silly mouss,
> 'How thou can fleit without feddir or fyn.'
>
> (29–30)

is the reaction of incorruptibility to the corruptible which became so in consequence of the fall of Adam, but still retains something of its original appearance. God made man in his own image; fallen man retains the likeness, but has much of the nature of beasts—or as the Prologue has it:

[1] Aquinas, *Summa Theologica* CXVIII. 3; LXXV. 6.

> Mony men in operatioun
> Ar lyk to beistis in thair conditioun
>
> (48–49)

Time is the natural habitat of beasts—in terms of the poem, they float with feathers and fins. Man's body has come to be subject to time, but still has no feathers or fins, only webbed ('lukkin') feet, the mark of Adam's fall. The corruption of the body is the paddock's 'fraud and als invy' (49), reflected in her ugly body, and the lower stylistic level adopted to describe it:

> The mouss beheld onto hir fronsyt face,
> Hir runclit beik, and hir lippis syd,
> Hir hyngand Browis and hir voce so hace,
> Hir logrand leggis and hir harsky hyd:
> Scho ran abak and on the paddok cryd,
> 'Gife I can any skeill of fysnomy,
> Thou hes sum pairte of fraud and als invy.'
>
> (43–49)

(One should notice the contrast between the mouse's learned language and that of the description which precedes it.) The paddock, in turn, blames Nature for her 'forme and qualite' (68). This echoes the Platonism of Chartres. It will be remembered that in the *Anticlaudianus*,[1] for instance, of Alan of Lille the soul is the only part of creation which does not come into Nature's power, limited as it was believed to the material universe. Unfallen man was the direct work of God, and Nature's master rather than her servant. The paddock (like Edmund in *King Lear*) recognizes Nature as his sole divinity, by whom he swears the 'murthour aith' that is so soon broken.

---

[1] Ed. R. Bossuat (Paris, 1955), ll. 62 ff.

> Scho golkit up and to the hevin can cry,
> 'Thou Jupiter, of natur god and king,
> I mak ane aith to the trewly that I
> This littill mouss sall our the wattir bring.'
>
> (92–95)

(d) *The Two Mice*

(*The Taill of the Uponlandis Mous, and the Burges Mous*)

The Two Mice is the first fable to have a particular reference
to fifteenth-century Scotland; it is built round the relationship
of the new Third Estate, the burgesses, to the stock from
which they sprang, the country folk, later symbolized by
Lindsay in the person of John the Commonweal.[1] Critics
unfortunately have tended to concentrate on animal rather
than human detail—especially as this is also the first of the
fables concerned with mice. Henryson's treatment of mice,
it may be said, is so particularly sympathetic that one is almost
forced to make such a choice.

> Till eik the cheir the surcharg furth scho brocht,
> A plait of groitis and a dische of meill;
> Threfe caikis als I trow scho sparit nocht
> Haboundantly about hir for to deill:
> Furmage full fyne scho brocht in steid of geill:
> A quhyt candill out of a coffer stall
> In steid of spyce to cresch thair teithis withall.
>
> (120–6)

The food described in these lines properly belongs to mice
(as also does the low stylistic level). The literary effect, how-

[1] John the Commonweal appears both in the *Dreme* (D. Hamer, *The Works
of Sir David Lindsay of the Mount*, Vol. 1 (S.T.S., 1931), pp. 4–38) and in *Ane
Satyre of the Thrie Estaitis* (Hamer, op. cit., Vol. 11).

ever, depends on the strictly human reference—surcharge, plate, dish; still more on the explicit human parallel twice introduced by the phrase *in steid of.* Nor is this parallel merely general, serving as it does to make the town mouse representative of a specific human class, the prosperous merchants of the burghs. (The country mouse has already been equated with the poor of the countryside.)

Again, the fact that the mice are blood relations has a self-evident meaning, in human rather than mouse terms.

> My moder said eftir that we wer borne,
> That ye and I lay baith within hir wame.
> I keip the ryt and custome of my deme,
> And of my ser, levand in povertie.
>
> (52–55)

The mice are children of the same parents, as are rich and poor humans. The underlying concept is almost John Ball's,

> When Adam dalf and Eve span,
> Who was then the gentleman?[1]

Part at least of the *Moralitas* proceeds from this level of interpretation.

> Blissit be symple lyfe withouttin dreid:
> Blissit be sobir feist in quiete:
> Quha hes ennuche, of no moir hes he neid,
> Thocht it be littill in to quantete.
>
> (212–15)

Over-ready sympathy with the mice may also obscure another aspect of the fable. Henryson found in his animals types not merely of humanity, but specifically of fallen humanity. This is as true of his mice as of his wolves and

[1] K. Sisam, *Fourteenth Century Verse and Prose* (Oxford, 1937), p. 152.

foxes. Thus, neither mouse has, in any legal sense, a right to
the houses in which they live, or to the food they eat. They
are like Everyman in the morality play in relation to his Goods.

> Landis haif we none of propirtie
>
> (56)

says the country to the town mouse, and indeed the fact has
been stressed from the beginning, most obviously for the rural
beast. She lives like an outlaw:

> The yungir wend up on land weill neir
> Rycht solitar, quhyle undir busk and breir,
> Quhyle in the corne in uthir menis schecht,
> As outlawis dois, and levis on thair wacht.
>
> (3–6)

Henryson's treatment of the other's status is more indirect
and ironic:

> The tothir mouss that in the burgh can byd
> Was gilt bruther and maid ane fre burgess,
> Tolefre alswa, but custome mair and less,
> And fredome had to ga quhair ever scho list
> Amang the cheiss and meill in ark and kist.
>
> (10–14)

The reference here is to the position of the merchant guilds,
which by the fifteenth century had frequently gained control
of Scottish burgh councils at the expense, administratively
and socially, of craftsmen, and to the privileges claimed by
their members. They were 'toll free'—that is, they did not
have to pay either the *magna custuma*, on the export of wool,
woolfells, and hides or the *parva custuma* on market goods
('custome mair and less').[1] But the effect is satiric. Henryson

[1] See Wood's note on p. 226 of his edition, and compare W. Croft Dickinson, op. cit., pp. 233 ff. Such exemption was very unusual.

implies that, like the mouse, the rich merchants are robbers, or at least pilferers. Elsewhere he has provided sufficient indication that the town mouse, as much as her sister, lives by theft.

> And in the samyn than went but mair abaid,
> Withouttin fyre or candill burnand bricht,
> *For commonly sic pykeris luvis nocht licht.*
>
> (40–42)

Compare too her guilty behaviour on the approach of the Spenser and the cat. There is nothing to correspond to this in either the Latin or French versions of the fable.

Romulus and *Ysopet* have contributed as little to another feature. The mice are most obviously types of fallen humanity, in their neglect of common Christian observance, a neglect which appears at different levels in different parts of the poem. Sometimes it is entirely linguistic. Easter and Lent, for instance, form the basis of metaphors which in effect are entirely secular

> My Gud Fryday is bettir nor your Pase
>
> (87)

says the town mouse, only to have her metaphor capped by her sister seventy lines later:

> I had levir thir fourty dayis fast
> With wattir caill or gnaw benis or peiss
> Than all your feist in this dreid & diseiss.
>
> (159–61)

Were it not for the 'haill Yule, haill!' of 128, the double reference to Eastertide, and especially '*thir* fourty dayis', might seem to suggest that Henryson visualized the action of his fable as developing over Easter. This cannot, I think, hold, but may serve to remind one of the comparison with another woman of the bourgeoisie, who, it will be remembered, was much given to jaunts and excursions, Chaucer's Wife of Bath:

> For evere yet I loved to be gay,
> And for to walke in March, Averill, and May,
> Fro hous to hous, to heere sondry talys.
>
> (D. 545–7)

The Wife of Bath had been on many pilgrimages. The burgess mouse dresses as a pilgrim when she goes to meet her sister. The comparison places the town mouse on the moral as well as the social scale. And, of course, as with the Wife, the references to Lent and Easter remain in effective contrast to the activities of the graceless mice.

On the level of action, the mice ask no blessing on their meal; (it will be noticed that nevertheless they wash before eating—a characteristic touch of the bourgeoisie).

> Withouttin grace thay wesche and went to meit.
>
> (107)

Similarly, on their arrival at the town mouse's home

> Without God speid thair harbery wes tane.
>
> (101)

This line too is echoed, and so emphasized and given importance, in a later part of the poem:

> Quhen in come Gib Huntar, our Joly Cat,
> And bad God speid—
>
> (165–6)

One may bring *Everyman* into comparison. The arrival of Gib Hunter is as shockingly unexpected as that of Death at the beginning of the play.[1]

---

[1] References are to the edition of A. C. Cawley (Manchester, 1961).

The Biblical overtones of the *Moralitas* chime with this
approach.

> O wantoun man quhilk usis for to feid
> Thy wame and makis it a god to be,
> Luke to thi self, I warne the weill on deid,
> The cat cumis, and to the mouss hevis e.
>
> (220–3)

The reference is to Philippians iii. 18–19, 'For many walk, of
whom I have told you often, and now tell you even weeping,
that they are the enemies of the cross of Christ: whose end is
destruction, whose god is their belly, and whose glory is in
their shame, who mind earthly things.' The enemies of the
cross of Christ whose end is destruction, are the mice in
relation, on the one hand, to Easter, on the other to Gib
Hunter and destruction.

Nor does this interpretation exhaust the potentialities of
the figure. The *Moralitas* is concerned with gluttony only
in so far as it appertains to pride and high position. 'Blythness
in hairt, with small possessioun' is the ideal presented in the
last line of the *Moralitas*, and contrasted to the perils under-
gone by those who trust themselves to the wheel of Fortune:

> As fitschis myngit ar with noble seid,
> So Intermellit is adversitie
> With erdly Joy, so that no stait is fre
> Without truble or sum vexatioun,
> And namely thay that clymis up most he,
> And nocht content of small possessioun.
>
> (206–11)

The emphasis here is on 'clymis', and in terms of adversity in
the fable, the reference is obviously not to the established
town mouse, but to her aspiring sister from the country. The

town mouse has her position and her security: not so her
sister:

> The burges had a hoill and in scho gois,
> Hir sistir had no place to hyd hir in.
>
> (136–7)

Thus it is the country mouse whom Gib Hunter catches, and
the description of his play with her, combines realistic
observation with verbal reminiscences of stock descriptions of
Fortune and her wheel:[1]

> Fra fute to fute scho kest hir to and fra,
> Quhyle up, quhyle doun, als tait as ony kid;
> Quhyle wald scho lat hir ryn undir the stra;
> Quhyle wald scho wynk and play with hir bukhid.
> Thus to the silly mouss grit harme scho did,
> Quhile at the last throw fair fortoun and hap
> Betwix the dressour and the wall scho crap.
>
> (169–75)

It is by 'fair fortoun and hap' that the mouse finally escapes.

If Gib Hunter is Fortune as well as Death, who is the
Spenser? It is tempting to apply the Boethian concept, and
suggest that he is the Providence which governs Fortune—a
suggestion which may gain some support from the etymo-
logical connexion of the word 'Spenser' with 'dispence' and
'dispensation'.

(e) The Sheep and the Dog
(The Taill of the Scheip and the Doig)

The effect of this *Taill* depends largely on a contrast at once
comic and sinister. On the one hand is the animal court with

---

[1] Compare, for instance, *The Frog and the Mouse*, 165–71 (quoted on
p. 113, above).

wolf as judge, raven as apparitor, fox as clerk, kite and vulture
as advocates. Satire of this kind forms part of the tradition of
the Beast-Epic, and in another context would not be taken
too seriously. Henryson, however, brings out the reality of
injustice, partly by making the court a Consistory, or ecclesiastical court, partly by developing the story in close conformity with the actual Scottish legal procedure of his day.[1] The
apparent unreality of the participants is thus combined with
considerable realism of procedure. Legal style is preserved.

> I, Maister Wolf, pairtles of fraud or gyle,
> Undir the panis of suspentioun
> And gret cursing and interdictioun,
> Sir Scheip, I chairge the straitly to compeir
> And answeir till a dog befoir me heir.
>
> (10–14)

The sheep is well aware of his rights under the law, and makes
his objections with precision

> Heir I declyne the juge, the tyme and place.

> This is my caus and motive in effect:
> The law sayis it is rycht perelouss
> Till interply befoir a Juge suspect;
> And thou, Ser Wolf hes ay bene odius
> To me, and with thyne tuskis revenus
> Hes slane full mony kynnismen of myne;
> Thairfoir, as Juge suspect, I the declyne.

> And schortly of this court the memberis all,

---

[1] See Wood's notes, pp. 240 ff. of his edition, and the references there
cited. It should be noticed that the sheep in the fable must represent a priest
who is subject to the ecclesiastical penalties threatened by the court. The word
Doig may conceal a reference to Doeg who slew the priest Ahimelech and his
companions (1 Samuel xxi. 7–xxii. 19). There may also be a reference to some-
one whose surname was Doig.

> Bayth assessouris, clerk and advocat,
> To me and myne ar ennemeis mortall,
> And ay hes bene, as mony scheiphird watt.
> This place as for the tyme is feriat
> In quhilk no Jugeis suld sit in consistory
> So lait at evin: I you accuss forthy.
>
> (42–56)

The judge reacts, not primarily as a wolf, but as a man of law, and the arbiters receive ironical praise for their devotion to their task—a devotion which involves hiding self-evident truth behind a cloud of learned comment.

> Off sevall mony volum thay revoll;
> The codyss and degestis new and ald:
> Prowe and contra strait argument thay resoll:
> Sum a doctrine, and sum ane other hald.
> For pryss nor prayer trow ye thay wald fald,
> Bot held the text and gloiss of the decreiss
> As trew Jugeis; I schrew thame that leiss.
>
> (71–77)

The implication is certainly of the letter that kills, and the word 'prayer' is significant. The arbiters would not 'fald' for righteous prayers any more than for unrighteous bribes. Henryson is careful to emphasize that there was no legal right of appeal from the decision of the arbiters. The consequence is the ruin of the sheep.

The theme, in other words, is Justice, and human injustice reveals itself in terms of the animal creation. The theme of the Prologue is repeated:

> mony men in operatioun
> Ar lyk to beistis in thair conditioun.
>
> (48–49)

One might compare the animal and bird names of characters in Ben Jonson's *Volpone*—Volpone, Corbaccio, Corvino, and the rest. Henryson's technique is almost the reverse of Jonson's, who uses animal names and the plot of Aesop's *Fox and Crow* to stress the bestial humours of his apparently human characters. Henryson's treatment of apparently animal characters in terms specifically human has the same final effect of highlighting human bestiality. Jonson too plays out his farce in terms of the law represented by the Venetian senators. But whereas *Volpone* concludes with at least a gesture towards conventional moral assumptions, Henryson allows the sheep no redress. The *Moralitas* ends with the unanswered prayer of the sheep (based, as Gregory Smith noted,[1] on Psalm xliv. 23).

> 'O Lord, quhy slypis thow so lang?
> Walk, and descerne my causs, groundit in richt.'
> (150–1)

Henryson's legal satire is made universal by the *Moralitas* which stands somewhat apart from all the other *Moralitates* of the *Fabillis*. Henryson scarcely pretends to offer such an allegorical interpretation of the events of the *Taill* as is found in *The Cock and the Jewel* or *The Frog and the Mouse*. That the sheep

> may present the figure
> Of pure commounis, that daylie ar opprest
> (113–14)

is to state the obvious; it is not in any recognized sense of the word allegory to state, for instance, of the raven, who has already been described as apparitor of the Consistory

---

[1] *Poems of Robert Henryson* (S.T.S., 1906–14), I. 22.

> This Revin I likin till a fals crownar,
> Quhilk hes a porteouss of the endytment,
> And passis furth befoir the Justice air,
> All misdoaris to bring till Jugement;
> Bot luke gife he be of a trew intent
> To skraip out Johine and wryt in Will or Wate,
> And so a bud at bayth the pairteis skat.

> (127–33)

Henryson does not interpret; rather he extends his satire to include Civil as well as Consistory courts—the entire machinery of the law during his time. Even in the *Moralitas*, however, the individual sufferer remains his chief concern; the Biblical complaint of the sheep, which makes no pretence of allegory, occupies five of the nine stanzas of the *Moralitas*.

(f) *The Wolf and the Lamb*
(*The Taill of the Wolf and the Lamb*)

The greater part of the *Taill* is occupied by a dialogue which, even when one recollects the stylistic conventions of the fable, remains strikingly unrealistic—particularly so in regard to the lamb. His three speeches seem wholly inappropriate to his age and situation. All are formal and indeed technical. The language of the first is that of natural philosophy and formal logic. In accordance with the *Prologue*, he proceeds by syllogism:

> Thocht I can nocht, Nature will me defend
> And of the deid perfyt experience:
> All hevie thing mone of the self discend,
> Bot gif sum thing on forss mak resistence:
> Thane may the streme be na wayis mak offens

> Na ryn bakwart; I drank beneth yow far;
> *Ergo* for me your drink is nevir the war.
>
> (29–35)

The language of the second, with its reference to Ezekiel xviii is scriptural and theological:

> Haif ye nocht hard quhat haly Scriptour sais,
> Dytit with the mouth of God Almycht?
> Off his awin deid ilk man salbeir the paiss,
> As pyne for syn, reward for werkis rycht.
> For my trespass quhy suld my sone haif plycht?
> Quha did the miss, lat thame sustene the pane.
>
> (50–55)

(Note the stylistic contrast with the words of the Wolf that follow:

> 'Ya,' quod the Wolf, 'yit plyis thou againe?')

The language of the third is legal:

> The law sayis, and ye will undirstand,
> Thair suld no man for wrang nor violenss,
> His adversar puneiss at his awin hand,
> Without process of law in audiens,
> Quhilk suld haif leif to mak lawchtfull defens,
> And thairupone summond peremptourly
> For to propone *contra* and reply.
>
> (64–70)

The lamb's words in general are absolutely precise—the technical language excludes ambiguity. He defends himself by irrefutable appeal, first to natural law, secondly to moral law, and thirdly to civil and canon law, the three systems on which human society is built.

To this, the language of the wolf is consciously opposed:

> 'Ha,' quod the Wolf, 'wald thou intruss ressoun
> Quhair wrang and reif suld dwell in properte?
> That is a poynt of oppin fals tressoun.'
>
> (78–80)

The wolf sets up 'wrang and reif' as opponents of the lamb's
Reason, but his use of the verb 'intruss' and of the phrase 'in
properte' has the paradoxical effect of making Reason appear
an alien quality disrupting the natural order of society, of
which the wolf takes himself to be the representative. Because
the wolf is speaking against the lamb's third argument, based
on civil and canon law, he exploits the legal connotations of
'intruss' and 'in properte'. In relationship to the lamb's other
speeches his technique is the same. The lamb's argument from
natural law, he characterizes as 'langaige outragius'. He caps
the lamb's quotation from Ezekiel with a twisted quotation
from Exodus xx. 5. Compare too the paradoxical use of the
words 'bald', 'fyle', and 'almouss' in the third stanza.

> 'How durst thou be so bald to fyle this bruke,
> Quhair I suld drink, with thy foull slavering?
> It wer almouss the for till draw and hing.'
>
> (17–19)

The wolf's concern is always to make right appear wrong
and wrong appear right.

The poem is thus a dialogue between the duplicity of the
wolf and the simplicity of the lamb:

> Quhill him thocht gude, presomyng thair nane ill.
>
> (13)

On a miniature scale, the action resembles the conflitc in
Book I of Spenser's *Faerie Queene* between Una with her

symbolic lamb and the false Duessa. It is characteristic of
Henryson's view of the world that he allows his wolf physical
victory despite dialectic defeat.

The *Moralitas*, like that of *The Sheep and the Dog*, is non-
allegorical. The *Taill* itself has an application that is wholly
general. The *Moralitas* is particular to Scotland, and within
Scotland to the rights and liabilities of the common man, and
in particular the tenant farmer.[1] In construction *Moralitas*
and *Taill* approximately correspond—both have a triple
division, marked in the *Taill* by the lamb's three speeches, in
the *Moralitas* by the threefold interpretation of the wolf. As
the third speech of the lamb was based on civil and canon law,
so the first wolf of the *Moralitas* is the Man of Law with his
'sutelte', 'nyss jympis and fraudis interkat', a perverter of the
law which the lamb had precisely expounded. Thereafter, however, the *Moralitas* moves almost completely away from the
action of the *Taill* and concerns itself entirely with unjust
dealings between landlord and tenant farmer:

> For Godis aw, how dar thou tak on hand,
> And thou in berne and byre so bene and big,
> To put him fra his tak and gar him thig?
>
> (117–19)

The different stylistic level of this compared to the language

---

[1] Cf. Dickinson, op. cit., p. 275, note 1: 'Short leases, or "tacks", of three or
five years were the curse of Scottish agriculture, and short leases for small
farmers were the rule until the "improvements" and "improving landlords" of
the eighteenth century. No tenant with a short lease would develop his land or
improve his buildings since, if he did so, the land, at the close of the lease,
might be let to another tenant or his own rent might be raised.' The first
quotation in the text refers to expulsion at the end of a lease, the second to
increased rent-service.

of the *Taill* should be noted—the familiar 'thou',[1] the expletive, the familiar and alliterative 'berne', 'byre', 'bene', 'big', the colloquial 'gar him thig'. Elsewhere in the *Moralitas* there is an abundance of humble detail:

> His horss, his meir he mone len to the laird
> To drug and draw in court and cariege:
> His servand or him self may nocht be spard
> To swynk & sweit withouttin meit or wage.
> Lo, as he standis in lawbour and boundage
> That skantly may he purchess by his maill
> To leif upone dry breid and wattir kaill.
>   (134–40)

Formally the *Moralitas* is Complaint or Satire, for which the appropriate stylistic level is low.

In most fables, the tale is an apparently specific series of events, which in the *Moralitas* receives an interpretation in general terms. *The Wolf and the Lamb* operates differently—the tale is given the widest possible reference, while the particular interpretation, with its markedly Scottish relevance, is reserved for the *Moralitas*.

(g) *The Cock and the Fox*
(*The Taill of Schir Chantecleir and the Foxe*)

The subject is Nobility, with its obverse Pride. Henryson's Chantecleir resembles the *grit lordis of Grew* in *Orpheus and Eurydice* 15. Their nobility was twofold, deriving partly from ancestry, partly from ability to keep ancestral standards:

---

[1] The wolf always addresses the lamb with the familiar, and indeed contemptuous, 'thou'; the lamb uses the polite 'ye' and 'you'.

> It is contrair the Lawis of nature
> A gentill man to be degenerat,
> Nocht following of his progenitour
> The worthe reull, and the lordly estait.
> (8–11)

There remains a difference, however. In *Orpheus*, because
Henryson treated his subject seriously, he was forced in some
measure to distance it, to view it at the double remove of
antiquity and allegory. The result is a certain inadequacy or
one-sidedness. In the *Taill*, on the other hand, by substituting
for a mythological demi-god a barnyard cock, he is able
to present very vividly the weaknesses of the ideal. Neither
version is complete without the other, as in another connexion
one might say that Chaucer's *Knight's Tale* is incomplete
without the *Miller's*, or equally that the *Miller's Tale* is incomplete without the *Knight's*.

It is chiefly by way of Lawrence the fox who tempts Chantecleir that Chantecleir's false nobility appears. Lawrence, of
course, wishes only to beguile; his instrument is flattery, and
the method he adopts is precisely the method of panegyric
stated by Henryson at the beginning of the *Orpheus*:

> The nobilnes and grit magnificens
> Of prince and lord, quhai list to magnifie,
> His ancestre and lineall discens
> Suld first extoll, and his genolegie,
> So that his harte he mycht inclyne thairby
> The moir to vertew and to worthiness
> Herand reherss his elderis gentilness. (1–7)

After the fox has established himself as Chantecleir's servant
('I come bot here, you[1] service for to mak', 42; 'Wald I nocht

---

[1] Note the fox's polite 'you'. The cock uses the condescending 'thou'.

serve you, ser, I wer to blame', 43; 'me, your servitour', 55),
he at once turns to Chantecleir's ancestors ('youre progenitouris', 44; compare the use of the word in *Orpheus*), and in
particular to Chantecleir's father, whom he presents with
ironic ambiguity as a generous lord who did not forget old
retainers (the fox obviously had eaten him). The fox establishes himself as a faithful servant with 'lyart lokkis', who
had been on intimate terms with the father, and who hopes to
reach the same intimacy with the son. He even addresses
Chantecleir as 'my fair sone'.

> Your fader oft fulfillit hes my wame
> And send me mete fra middingis to the muris;
> At his ending I did my besy curis
> To hald his hede and gife him drinkis warme:
> Syne at the last that swete swelt in my arme.
>
> (45–49)

So far as I am aware, there is no parallel to this superbly
hypocritical use of 'swete', strengthened as it is by the alliteration with 'swelt', in the entire range of Henryson's works.
The fox is a pious as well as a faithful servant, who contrives
to suggest discreetly that he is in holy orders. He sang the
Dirige over the cock's dead father, and he interlards his speech
with mild clerical oaths ('Be my saull', 40; 'Be my saule, and
the blissit Sacrament', 59), which suggest sincerity by their
very harmlessness. He does not neglect Chantecleir's outward
signs of nobility:

> Your breste, your beke, your hekill and your came.
>
> (58)

Nor is he afraid to exploit the potentialities of an ambiguous
servility.

> You for to serve I wald crepe on my wame
> In frost and snaw, in wederis wan and wete,
> And lay my lyart lokkis under your fete.
>
> (61–63)

One should not miss the smooth effect of the alliteration on *w*, *f*, and *l*.

Lawrence's purpose in praising Chantecleir's father corresponds to the prescription found in the *Orpheus*. It is to encourage the cock to emulation. Degeneracy is the disastrous possibility inherent in the concept of nobility. Once Lawrence has established himself in the part of hereditary retainer, he is quick to hint that Chantecleir is not the cock his father was. As the degeneracy of Orpheus showed in his music, so, the fox suggests, does that of Chantecleir:

> Me think you changit and degenerate
> Fra your fader and his conditioun:
> Off crafty crawing he mycht bere the croun:
> For he wald on his tais stand and crawe.
>
> (66–69)

So later when Chantecleir has proved that he can crow, the fox still makes a single reservation:

> He wald, and haif na dout,
> Bayth wink and craw and turne him thryis about.
>
> (76–77)

Lawrence induces in Chantecleir a state of euphoria by the smoothness and ambiguous apparent simplicity of his approach, combined as it is with the occasional use of an impressive Latin term, like 'servitour', 'progenitouris', or 'degenerate'. The sudden intrusion of reality is indicated by an abrupt change of diction to the harshly monosyllabic:

> And suddanlie, or he had sung ane note,
> The Fox was war and hynt him be the throte.
>
> (83–84)

The *Moralitas* confirms that Henryson intended this section at least of the fable as a comment on what may be termed the rhetorical concept of nobility. This is more obviously true of the cock:

> Till oure purpois this cok wele may we call
> A nyce proud man, void and vanegloriouss,
> Off kyn or gude quhilk is presumptuouss.
>
> (194–6)

Equally however it is the false rhetoric of the fox on which Henryson comments:

> This feynit fox may wele be figurate
> To flatteraris with plesand wirdis quhite,
> With fals menyng and mouth mellifluate,
> To loife and lee quhilk settis thair delyte.
>
> (204–7)

One should particularly notice the unexpected alliterative linking, *to loife and lee*—unexpected in terms both of meaning and the past history of the verb *loife*. *Loife* is derived from Old English *lofian*, 'to praise', *lof*, 'praise, glory', a word with almost entirely heroic connotations. Beowulf, for instance, is described as *lofgeornost*, 'most eager for praise, glory'. 'The reference', says Klaeber, 'is either to deeds of valour . . . or to the king's liberality toward his men'. In older use at least, there is nothing pejorative about the term. Henryson must, I think, have intended a deliberate clash with the normal associations of the word, a clash which is central to his intention in the fable.

Henryson effects the transition to the second part of the fable by methods which combine realism with courtly convention. The widow's immediate reaction to the theft is made more or less appropriate both to her assumed social level, and the style previously adopted by Henryson. Only the beating of the breast may seem a little excessive. Her subsequent swoon changes the style to a less realistic, more courtly level:

> As scho war wod, with monye yell and cry
> Ryvand hir hair, upoun hir breist can bete;
> Syne paill of hew, half in ane extasye,
> Fel doun for cair in swoning and in swete.
>
> (92–95)

Stylistically, her swoon belongs almost to the world of the *Testament*, and Cresseid's swoon in her oratory. Like that, too, it is followed by a debate or parliament, with the important difference that the parliament is not one of planetary deities, but of hens. It is perhaps worth while to quote Charles Muscatine[1] on passages of this kind in twelfth- and thirteenth-century French courtly romance.

'Extraordinary emotions have their appropriate actions and gestures. Sorrow, for instance, is accompanied by sinking of the head, weeping and sighing, failure of the voice and swooning, and more passionate gestures, as wringing and beating the hands, striking and scratching the face, pulling on hair and beard, ripping garments, and so forth. Again the modern reader must be careful not to look at these apparently crudely described motions for physiological accuracy—though some may be accurate enough, for all we know—or for refined

---

[1] *Chaucer and the French Tradition* (Berkeley and Los Angeles, 1957), p. 29.

discrimination of tone. When the *Eneas* poet writes, as he
often does,

> *A icest mot perdi l'aloine*
> *et pasma soi . . .*

(With this her breathing failed and she fainted.)
he is indicating an emotional climax, but we must not expect
him to deal with it in realistic, medical terms. Like the poetic-
ally elevated speech which often precedes or follows it, this
kind of action has only an emblematic relation to the facts of
life. It is like the patterned and formal gestures that must have
accompanied Greek tragedy, for which the condition of per-
formance would seem to have made naturalistic subtleties of
action impossible.'

The *Testament of Cresseid* proves that Henryson knew and
exploited the convention described by Muscatine. In all probability, that is to say, the fact that Pertok's lament, a poetic-
ally elevated speech, follows the widow's swoon, shows that
Henryson intended his poem to be read in terms of the same
convention. The critic's problem is the emblematic relationship borne by speech and swoon to the fable as a whole.
There are several possibilities.

In the first place, the plot of the fable demands a certain
rehabilitation of Chantecleir after his fall to the flattery of the
fox. Unlike the cock in *The Taill of the Cok and the Jasp*,
Chantecleir is not a fool: he can use his wits to rescue himself
even from the fox's mouth. On one level the widow's swoon,
appropriate as it is to the death of a courtly hero, serves to
re-elevate Chantecleir to something of the height from which
the fox had dethroned him.

Against this one may urge that the heightening of style

and convention serves only as a prelude to a second deflation
of Chantecleir in the remarks of Sprutok and Coppok, and in
Pertok's revision of her first opinion. The deflation, however,
is not so much of the individual Chantecleir, as of the general
rhetorical concept of nobility which Chantecleir embodies.
The widow and Pertok both react somewhat absurdly, but in
accordance with the courtly code. In particular, the hypocritical series of sentimental rhetorical questions in which
Pertok phrases her lament bring out the absurdity of the
entire situation—not least when the cock is still alive. One
should compare the laments of Orpheus and Cresseid, neither
of which is to be taken entirely at face value. The reader's
sense of uneasiness is at once confirmed by Sprutok's down-
to-earth retort.

> 'Seiss, sister, of your sorrow:
> Ye be to made for him sic murning maiss.
> We sall fair weill, I find sanct Johne to borrow:
> The proverb sayis as guid luif cumis as gaiss.'
>
> (113–16)

A reconciliation of these somewhat opposed points of view
is perhaps to be found in a third approach. The widow and
Pertok act in the conventionally noble fashion. Sprutok leads
a reaction, and is followed by Pertok, while Coppok adds a
condemnation of Chantecleir's entire life. The human terms,
however, in which the condemnation is expressed are as inappropriate to the death of a cock as was the earlier eulogy.
It is a hen who says in terms reminiscent of the Wife of Bath,

> I will put on my hellye dayis clais
> And mak me fresch aganis this Jolye May,
> Syne chant this sang *Was nevir wedow so gay.*
>
> (117–19)

In terms of hens this is absurd, and in human terms Sprutok merely substitutes fabliau conventions for those of romance. Coppok too introduces alien and inappropriate standards:

> Yone was ane verrye veangeance fra the hevin:
> He was sa loweouss and so licherouss,
> Seiss coud he nocht with sissokkis mo than sevin.
> Bot rychtuous God, haldand the ballanais evin,
> Smytis full soir, thocht he be patient,
> Adulteraris that list thame nocht repent.
>
> (135–40)

A cock's polygamy, after all, is not to be judged on the same terms as a man's, and Coppok herself was one of the 'sissokkis'. The effect is one not of justice but of arbitrariness— the arbitrariness of posthumous reputation in relation to such an ideal of nobility as is represented by Chantecleir. I have used *Orpheus and Eurydice* to illustrate the ideal; posthumous fame, however, which in that poem remains inconspicuous, certainly formed part of the ideal, and Henryson's approach in the fable is perhaps best illustrated by the comparison with Book III of Chaucer's *House of Fame*. Chantecleir deserves Pertok's first lament to the extent that the sixth company to approach the goddess deserves the fame it obtains:

> They seyden: 'Mercy, lady dere!
> To tellen certeyn as hyt is,
> We han don neither that ne this,
> But ydel al oure lyf ybe.
> But, natheles, yet preye we
> That we mowe han as good a fame,
> And gret renoun and knowen name,
> As they that han doon noble gestes.' . . .

'I graunte,' quod she, 'be my trouthe!'
                    (1730–7; 1763)

Coppok's reaction is like that of the goddess to the seventh company:

> Thoo come the seventh route anoon,
> And fell on knees everychoon,
> And seyde, 'Lady, graunte us sone
> The same thing, the same bone,
> That ye this nexte folk han doon.'
> 'Fy on yow', quod she, 'everychon!
> Ye masty swyn, ye ydel wrechches,
> Ful of roten, slowe techches!
> What? false theves! where ye wolde
> Be famous good, and nothing nolde
> Deserve why, ne never ye roughte?
> Men rather yow to hangen oughte!'
>   (1771–82)

Henryson's charity appears in one feature. The fame sought by Chaucer's companies is genuinely posthumous; the award of Fame is permanent. Chantecleir receives both kinds of posthumous fame, but at the end he survives to say:

> I was unwyis that winkit at thy will
> Quhairthrow allmaist I lossit had my heid.
>   (183–4)

The poem ends with the sanity of Chantecleir's return to the barnyard:

> With that the coke our feildis tuke the flicht;
> In at the wedowis levar coud he licht.
>   (188–9)

(h) The Fox and the Wolf

(The Taill how this foirsaid Tod maid his Confessioun to Freir Wolf Waitskaith)

Henryson built this fable round a single comic episode, that in which Lawrence transforms the kid into a salmon by drowning it, and so fraudulently evades his vow to abstain from meat. As is shown elsewhere,[1] his model may have been Fable XLVII, which appears in some manuscripts of the *Romulus* of Gualterus Anglicus. In Gualterus, however, the characters differ; they are a wolf who has vowed to abstain from meat, and a lamb whom he kills and eats as salmon. The fable contains only this single episode. Henryson has not only changed the characters; he has added the astrological warning given to Lawrence, the episode of the confession made to the wolf, and Lawrence's death. He has also linked the story to that of *The Cock and the Fox* which precedes it, and *The Trial of the Fox* which follows. As a whole, his poem is considerably more elaborate, even symphonic, than the Latin, and the elaboration—particularly in terms of the astrological *motif* introduced by Henryson—is not unrelated to the *Orpheus and Eurydice* and the *Testament of Cresseid*.

From the beginning of the fable, Lawrence obviously regards himself as a nocturnal creature, to whose thieving activities daylight is hostile, night favourable. During the day he lies low, and it is only when the sun has set and Venus shows her 'lustye visage' that he ventures from his den. If one allows for differences of tone and stylistic level between fable and tragedy, the opening recalls that of the *Testament of*

[1] See Appendix III.

Cresseid, which also begins with the apparent triumph of
night over day, Venus over Phoebus, the appetitive over the
rational. In the *Testament* natural order begins to be restored
by the parliament of the seven planets, and much the same
happens in *The Fox and the Wolf*. When Lawrence looks at the
night sky his innate knowledge of astrology teaches him that
the night is as hostile to his activities as was the day. His
horoscope is not entirely hopeless: the favourable Jupiter,
for instance, is in his own house, Sagittarius. Saturn, however,
the greater infortune, is in a position of particular power; he
is in his house Capricorn, and at the same time, because his
other house, Aquarius, is the ascendant, Saturn is Lord of the
Ascendant. (Capricorn, it should be noted, is the Goat, and
it is Lawrence's theft of a kid which leads to his death; Jupiter
is in Sagittarius, the Archer, and Lawrence is killed by an
arrow; it is perhaps also significant that Mercury is in his
exaltation in Virgo, and that Virgo has power over the abdo-
men, diaphragm, and intestines, the appetitive organs pierced
by the goatherd's arrow.) It is probably the position of Saturn
which leads to Lawrence's outburst:

> 'Allace', quod he, 'rycht waryit ar we thevis;
> Our lyfe is sett ilk nycht in avinture:
> Our cursit craft full mony ane mischevis,
> For evir we steill and evir alyk ar pure.
> In dreid and schame our dayis we indure,
> And widdynek and crakraip callit als,
> And syne till our hyre ar hangit be the hals.'
>
> (43–49)

His speech, it should be noted, is one of self-pity, not of
penitence, and otherwise is chiefly notable for the assumption

that theft is an ordinary honest trade pursued under conditions of unusual difficulty. It is clear that Lawrence has no rational grasp of the realities of his position. Nevertheless, the astrological warning makes him at least attempt to make his peace with God by the sacrament of penance—the confession which forms the second episode of the tale, and which forms the main subject of the *Moralitas*.

Self-centredness reappears in Lawrence's choice of confessor—the wolf, to whom here and in *The Trial of the Fox* Henryson has given holy orders. Significantly he is not merely a priest, he is a friar, Freir Wolf Waitskath, and specifically a Franciscan, as is shown by his 'rousett coull of gray'. (His 'paill and petouss face' forms a nice additional touch.) Henryson is probably taking advantage of the popular belief that friars had greater power of confession, and gave easier penance than the secular clergy, a belief most easily illustrated by Chaucer's portrait of the Friar in the *General Prologue* to the *Canterbury Tales*.[1] Certainly the wolf's absolution is easily obtained, although not perhaps quite so easily as the modern reader might suppose. The three parts of the sacrament of penance are *Contritio*, *Confessio*, and *Satisfactio*, and when the wolf says to Lawrence,

> 'Thou wantis pontis twa
> Belangand to perfyt confessioun:
> Now to the thrid pairte of pennance lat us ga'
>   (99–101)

it is natural to suppose that he refers to *Contritio* and *Confessio*. As on this assumption Lawrence is found wanting in *Satisfactio* also, the wolf appears to absolve him on no grounds

[1] 218 ff.

whatever. This is to go too far. Henryson does not indicate that anything was wanting in the fox's *Confessio*—indeed he goes out of his way to treat the seal of confession seriously:

> Quhen I thus saw, I drew a littill by,
> For it effeiris nowdir to heir nor spy,
> Nor to reveill thing said undir that sele.
>
> (81–83)

As indicated by the wolf's questions, the 'pontis twa' seem rather to be contrition and forbearance, in both of which Lawrence is lacking; the third is 'pane', *poena*, which Lawrence is prepared to accept, provided that it is light. Lawrence, in fact, lacks two of the four rather than three of the three points of confession—a lack which leaves the absolution something short of difficult, but not entirely gratuitous.

Even so, Lawrence might have escaped his fate. When in the course of the sacrament he says

> 'I Schame to thig, I can nocht wirk, ye wat'
>
> (97)

he is echoing the words of the unjust steward in Luke xvi. 3 —the unjust steward, it will be remembered, who regained his lord's favour by making himself a friend of the mammon of unrighteousness. Lawrence obviously plans a similar course, which fails as a result of his ingenious stupidity in the episode of the salmon.

(i) *The Trial of the Fox*

(The Taill of the Sone and Air of the foirsaid Foxe, callit Father wer: Alswa the Parliament of fourfuttit Beistis, haldin be the Lyoun)

The most obvious quality of *The Trial of the Fox* is an ironic comic vigour, not unlike that found in some plays of the Wakefield cycle, and most elaborately developed in the episode of the red cap by which the wolf is made Doctor of Divinity. Other instances are the 'faderlye pitee' which makes the fox bury his father's naked body in a peat-pot, a hole in a bog, and the steps which he takes to avoid recognition at the lion's parliament:

> His hude he drew far doun attour his ene,
> And wynkand with the ane E furth can wend:
> Clyncheand he come that he suld nocht be kend,
> And for dreddour that he suld thoill areist
> He playit bukhud anone fra beist to beist.

(171–5)

Comic vigour, unfortunately, has combined with textual corruption to obscure the religious and political significance which to Henryson, no doubt, was the main justification for the tale. Yet the likelihood of a particular political significance is at once evident in terms of the precision with which the lion's parliament is described. It is a Scottish parliament, summoned by Unicorn Pursuivant, and fenced by the panther. The fox is eventually hanged, not because he murdered the lamb, but because he broke the king's peace proclaimed at the opening of parliament. All the animal estates compear, with the exception of the grey mare, who is proclaimed *contumax*. The wolf, who is the king's ambassador, is appropriately a master of chancery hand and style. The mare alleges a privilege. All the terms of the description in fact show the same legal precision.

Two instances of textual corruption found in all sources other than Bannatyne have done most to obscure Henryson's central reference, which is religious rather than political. To John Leslie,[1] the Roman Catholic bishop of Ross from 1565 to 1596, Henryson's time marked the beginning of a decline in the monastic life of Scotland, a decline whose origins he connected with Dunfermline Abbey, and with Henry Crichton, whom in 1468 James III intruded as abbot in place of Alexander Thomson who had been duly elected by the monks. 'From this proceidet the first and foul sklander that efter infected monasteries and Mounckis throuch al Scotland.' James's reign certainly saw an increased tension between Church and Crown, which is further illustrated by the struggle between the king and Patrick Graham, first archbishop of St. Andrews, which led to the latter's confinement in Dunfermline and elsewhere after his deposition in 1478. Parliament also became involved; in 1469 and 1471 the Estates enacted that abbeys which had not previously been provided from Rome should not be purchased there, and in 1482 and 1484 the acts against barratry were renewed.[2] Henryson must have been aware of those developments, and the Bannatyne text makes it clear that it is against this background that *The Trial of the Fox* should be read. As I have shown, the parliament of the tale is the Scottish parliament, and heraldry

---

[1] *Historie of Scotland, translated in Scottish by Father James Dalrymple,* Vol. II (S.T.S., 1895), pp. 90–91.
[2] Croft Dickinson, op. cit., p. 268.

makes it plain that the lion is the king of Scotland, enthroned
with sceptre, sword and crown, as on the Scottish arms. The
three leopards who serve him are those of England, and when
the lion says:

> I Lat you wit my mycht is merceabill
> And steris none that ar to me prostrat,
>
> (134–5)

he is adapting the motto of the kings of Scotland, *Parcere
prostratis scit nobilis ira leonis.*[1] The full point, however, is
established by the significance given to the mare and the fox
only in Bannatyne. The mare represents the religious orders:

> This mere is men of contemplatioun,
> Off pennance walkand in this wildernace,
> As monkis and othir men of religioun.
>
> (302–4)

The fox is the temptation for them to return to life in the
world, represented by the lion himself:

> This tod I likin to temptatioun
> Berand to mynd monye thochtis vane,
> That daylie sagis men of religioun
> Cryand to thame, 'Cum to the warld agane.'
>
> (323–6)

The wolf who is kicked by the mare represents sensuality—
the incontinence, in all probability, of many churchmen,
which had become a notorious scandal, and which for instance,
had recently received particular condemnation in the decree
De Concubinariis of the Council of Basle.[2]

[1] Compare Wood's notes on pp. 234 and 238 of his edition, and the note by
Bruce Dickins in *The Times Literary Supplement*, 21 February 1924.

[2] I single out this decree chiefly because it is quoted verbatim in the General
Statutes of the Provincial Council of the Scottish Church held at Edinburgh

Relations between James and the Scottish church thus give significance to the central action of the tale. At the same time, these relations formed part of a larger European pattern of which Henryson may have been aware. In the body of the fable the lion represents James III; in the *Moralitas* his significance is more general:

> The Lyon is this warld be liklynace
> To quhom lowtis bayth Emperour and king.
>
> (295–6)

In the context of the 1480s, the word Emperor can refer only to the Holy Roman Emperor who at that time was Frederick III, whose character in some ways resembled that of James III, and whose relationship to the papacy was often strained. It was during Frederick's reign, for instance, that Constantinople fell, and later, when he gave only lukewarm support to Pius II's scheme for a crusade against the Turks, the Pope wrote to him: 'How can you be called the protector and advocate of the Church when you not only desert the Church but slight the very religion and faith of Christ?'[1] The dispute between Pius and Diether von Isenburg, Archbishop-Elector of Mainz, also belongs to Frederick's reign. The comparison of Frederick and James seems to recur in the rather different, non-ecclesiastical context of *The Lion and the Mouse*:

> As I suppoiss, this mychty gay lyoun
> May signify a prince or empriour,

as late as 1549 (D. Patrick (editor), *Statutes of the Scottish Church*, Scottish History Society, 1907, pp. 89–91).

[1] I quote the translation and abridgement of the *Commentaries of Pius II* made by F. A. Gragg and L. C. Gabel and published as *Memoirs of a Renaissance Pope* (New York, 1962), p. 125.

A potestat or yit a king with croun
Quhilk suld be walkryfe gyd and govirnour
Of his peple, and takis no laubour
To rewll nor steir the land nor justice keip,
Bot lyis still in lustis, slewth and sleip.

(253–9)

Henryson, in other words, may have been aware of a general
movement in Europe which found particular embodiment in
Scotland and Germany, and which became the object of his
satire in this fable. Very probably a contemporary audience
would have been able to find precise identifications for more
than one of the characters of the tale. In particular the bastard
and illiterate fox gives an impression of individuality which
may well have had a basis in one of the illegitimate sons of
Scottish noblemen irregularly and disastrously promoted
to a major ecclesiastical benefice.

(j) *The Preaching of the Swallow*
(*The Preiching of the Swallow*)

This is the most complex and in some ways the most reward-
ing of the *Fabillis*. The theological and philosophic Prologue
merges almost imperceptibly into the fable proper with its
emphasis on human folly and weakness as represented by the
birds; the *Moralitas* shows the same themes which it links
directly to sin and damnation. The structure of the poem
resembles the landscape of *Piers Plowman*—on the one hand
God, on the other Satan, and between Middle Earth, the Field
full of folk, with its potentiality of redemption and damnation. But the poems differ in that Henryson primarily sees the

potentiality in intellectual, and indeed philosophical, terms:
his approach is nearer to that of Boethius and some among
the Schoolmen in the emphasis which it lays on the intellectual rather than the revealed understanding of salvation and
damnation; the theology is primarily rational and natural,
although there is no confusion of spiritual and material.

The emphasis throughout is on man's intellect in relation
to divine Providence—'the profound wit of God omnipotent' (2). Verbally, this theme dominates, sometimes in phrases
that emphasize the divine *rationale*— 'God in all his warkis
wittie is' (42)—although more often the emphasis falls on
imperfect humanity. Henryson makes much use of proverbs,
sententiae, of which the proper use of time tends to be the
recurrent theme—'It is grite wissdome to provyde before'
(118), '*Nam levius ledit quicquid prævidimus ante*' (133), 'wo
is him can nocht be war in tyme' (168). The central relationship of human to divine providence is described in terms
which recall the *Kingis Quair*[1]—indeed in a sense the entire
fable is an expansion of two stanzas from that speech of
Minerva to the dreamer upon which so much of the *Quair*
depends.

> And quhare a persone has tofore knawing
>   Off it that is to fall purposly,
> Lo, fortune is bot wayke in suich a thing,
>   Thou may wele wit, and here ensample quhy;
>   To God, that is the first caus onely
> Off every thing, there may no fortune fall
> And quhy? for he foreknawin is of all.

[1] Ed. W. Mackay Mackenzie (London, 1939). Compare also my article
'Tradition and the Interpretation of the *Kingis Quair*', to which I refer in
Chapter I, p. 15, n. 2.

And therfore thus I say to this sentence:
   Fortune is most and strangest evermore,
Quhare leste foreknawing or intelligence
   Is in the man; and, sone, of wit or lore
   Sen thou art wayke and feble, lo, therfore,
The more thou art in dangere and commune
With hir, that clerkis clepen so Fortune.

                (stanzas 148–9)

To this the closest verbal parallel occurs at the beginning of
the fable, and one cannot but remark how far Henryson's
verse excels that of James as a vehicle for theological exposition.

> The he prudence and wirking mervellus,
> The profound wit of God omnipotent,
> Is so perfyt and so ingenius,
> Excelland fer al manis argument,
> For quhy till him all thing is ay present,
> Rycht as it is, or ony time salbe,
> Befoir the sicht of his devinite.

                (1–7)

Fable and *Quair* also resemble each other in their discussion of the place of human intellect in the hierarchy. They
share the belief that in some measure the human mind can
partake of divine foreknowledge. To James the wise man is
superior to Fortune. For Henryson the same possibility presents itself under two aspects. The secrets of the Trinity are
inaccessible to natural reason, but some knowledge of God
may be obtained from his creation:

> Yit nevirtheles we may have knawlegeing
> Off God Almychtie be his creatouris.

                (28–29)

Accordingly, by his knowledge of the natural world, the swallow is able to foretell the ill fortune of the other birds at the hands of the fowler. Fortune, a figure central to the *Quair*, does not appear in the fable, but her place is taken by the fowler. Even for this, however, there is some verbal precedent in stanza 135 of the *Quair*:

> For as the fouler quhistlith in his throte
>   Diversly, to counterfete the brid,
> And feynis mony a suete and strange note
>   Till sche be fast lokin his net amyd
>   That in the busk for his desate is hid,
> Ryght so the fatour, the fals theif, I say,
> With suete tresoun oft wynnith thus his pray.

The intermediary between this stanza and the fable is very possibly the episode of Lydgate's *Pilgrimage of the Life of Man*[1] in which the pilgrim finds his way blocked by the nets of Satan. One might also compare a couplet from the *Moralitas* of *The Fox, the Wolf and the Husbandman*:

> For Mammon may be callit the Devillis net,
> Quhilk Sathanas for all sinfull hes set.
>
> (2444–5)

The literary references of the fable, however, are not confined to works of the fifteenth century. The concept of the fowler, for instance is ultimately biblical; the most probable source being the seventh verse of the 123rd Psalm (Ps. 124, A.V.) 'Anima nostra sicut passer erepta est de laqueo venantium; laqueus contritus est, et nos liberati sumus'. This is only one of many possible biblical analogues; compare for

---

[1] Ed. F. J. Furnivall and K. B. Locock, E.E.T.S. LXXVII, LXXXIII XCII (1899, 1901, 1904), lines 18999–19410.

instance Proverbs vii. 23 'Donec transfigat sagitta jecur ejus; velut si avis festinet ad laqueum, et nescit quod de periculo animae illius agitur', or Ecclesiastes ix. 12 'Nescit homo finem suum; sed sicut pisces capiuntur hamo, et sicut aves laqueo comprehenduntur, sic capiuntur homines in tempore malo, cum eis extemplo supervenerit.' Secular references must also be noted. The relationship of soul and body is seen mostly in Platonic but partly in Aristotelian terms; for Henryson as for Plato[1] the body is the prison of the soul in which the spiritual faculties are blinded.

> Oure mirk and deidlye corss materiale
> Blindis the spiritual operatioun,
> Lyke as man war bundin in presoun.
>
> (12–14)

The blinding force is 'sensualitie', the result of which is to oppress the soul with 'phantesye' as opposed to reason. Henryson assumes the division of the brain into three cells, the front assigned to fantasy, the middle to reason, and the back to memory. Compare in *Orpheus and Eurydice* the interpretation of Orpheus:

> Quhilk callit is the pairte intelletyfe
> Off manis saule, and undirstanding fre,
> And seperat fra sensualitie.
> Euridices is our effectioun,
> Be fantesy oft movit up and doun;
> Quhile to ressone it castis the delyte,
> Quhyle to the flesche it settis the appetyte
>
> (428–34)

and the phraseology of the *Testament*

---

[1] *Gorgias*, 493a; *Phaedo* 62b: 66c.

The Idole of ane thing, in cace may be
Sa deip Imprentit in the fantasy
That it deludis the wittis outwardly.

(507–9)

Aristotle[1] provides the image of the bat's eye—an image which became a commonplace, although it should be noted that Henryson's use comes very close in context to Aristotle's own. The concept of God seeing all time as perpetually present is Boethian, and the latter part of the prologue is based partly on Boethius, partly on scholastic philosophy and devotion. Here the Victorines are perhaps of first importance. As has already been noted, Henryson deduces the attributes of the Creator from creation. This was a particularly Victorine subject of meditation. 'A more speculative school of devotion was associated with the Augustinian Canons of the abbey of St. Victor in France, and particularly with the German Hugh of St. Victor (*c.* 1096–1141) and the Scot, Richard of St. Victor (d. 1173), who made their characteristic schemes of meditation depend in the first place upon the contemplation of the harmony of the universe. God is to be loved for his gifts and benefits. Man has been placed at the apex of the natural creation and all creation has been designed to provide insight which can lead men to the love of God.'[2] A fairly specific parallel to Henryson occurs in Hugh of St. Victor's *De Sacramentis* I. ii. 13. 'Et inventa est in tribus his Trinitas ineffabilis quae in Creatore quidem unum sunt, sed per creaturae speciem divisim se ad cognitionem effundunt.

---

[1] *Metaphysics* II (α), Chapter I. The same figure is quoted, for example, by Vincent of Beauvais, *De Eruditione Filiorum Nobilium IV* (ed. A. Steiner, Cambridge, Mass., 1938).

[2] G. Shepherd (ed.), *Ancrene Wisse* (London and Edinburgh, 1959), p. l.

Suscepit enim formam potestatis rerum immensitas; sapientiae
pulchritudo, bonitatis utilitas.' For Henryson, too, the Trinity
is ineffable, but has attributes which are to be discovered in
creation:

> For God is in his power infinyte,
> And mannis saule is febill and owir small,
> Off undirstanding waik and unperfyte,
> To comprehend him that contenis all.
> Non suld presume be reasoun naturale
> To serche the secretis of the Trinetie,
> Bot trow fermlie and lat dirk ressounis be.
>
> Yit nevirtheles we may have knawlegeing
> Off God Almychtie be his creatouris.
>
> (22–30)

Here, perhaps, there is also a direct reference to Aquinas, who
in some measure was opposed to the methods of Victorine
theology. The last three lines of the first stanza come close to
Summa Theologica XXXII. 1. 'It is impossible to attain to the
knowledge of the Trinity by natural reason—but not what
belongs to the distinction of the persons.' At the same time
Henryson without the precision of Hugh sees something of
the Trinity in creation. The infinite power of God is assumed.
Henryson is concerned first with Wisdom, and secondly with
Goodness. The wisdom of God is proved by the harmony
of the material creation (*sapientiae pulchritudo*); the firmament,
the spheres, and the four elements of the lower world. The
fairness of God is proved by the beauty of the animal creation,
and particularly of man, made in God's image. The goodness
and benignity of God is proved by his subjection of the
creation to man's use (*bonitatis utilitas*):

All creatouris he maid ffor the behuiffe
Off man, and till his suppertatioun,
Into this erd baith under and above
In nowmer, wecht and dew proportioun.
                    (50–53)

By 'creature' Henryson understands the material as well as the animate creation, and he illustrates the benignity of God primarily in terms of the revolution of the seasons. In this he returns to the Boethian tradition as in *O stelliferi conditor orbis*:[1]

Tu frondifluae frigore brumae
Stringis lucem breviore mora:
Tu, cum fervida venerit aestas,
Agiles nocti dividis horas.
Tua vis varium temperat annum
Ut quas Boreae spiritus aufert
Revehat mites Zephyrus frondes,
Quaeque Arcturus semina vidit
Sirius altas urat segetes.

Professor Kinsley describes[2] the portraits of the four seasons as an 'ornate conventional pageant', only excepting the description of winter. But in the first place, the portraits are more than merely a pageant—they form an organic part of the argument of the prologue, and at the same time prepare for the main action of the fable, the stages of which are marked by the procession of the seasons. Because it so successfully reveals this connexion, the transition from prologue to fable is one of the most brilliant things in Henryson. In the prologue spring is described last and in effect it is into the

---

[1] *Consolatio* I, Metrum 5.
[2] *Scottish Poetry, A Critical Survey* (London, 1955), p. 20.

description that the poet walks to experience the action. Three words are enough:

> *That samin seasoun* into a soft morning,
> Rycht blyith thai bitter blastis wer ago,
> Unto the wod to see the flouris spring
> And heir the mavissis sing and birdis mo,
> I passit furth.
>
> (92–96)

Secondly, Professor Kinsley assumed that the description of winter is realistic not conventional. But one term need not exclude the other, and that an element of convention exists in the description of winter may be established by a comparison with the descriptions of winter weather, for instance, in *Sir Gawain and the Green Knight.*[1]

Finally, it may well be that details in the portraits of summer and spring are conventional, even in a pejorative sense. The mantle of Flora is not an original concept, nor are mavis, merle, and lark unusual as typical birds of spring. On the other hand, I suggest that there is much originality in other parts of the same description—the precision, for instance, of 'stilland' in the line

> With heat and mosture stilland fra the skye,
>
> (63)

the metaphor used to describe Spring

> The secretare of Somer with his seill,
>
> (86)

or the combination of 'columbie', 'kikis', and 'clay' in

[1] See especially 726 ff. (ed. of J. R. R. Tolkien and E. V. Gordon, Oxford, 1925).

> Quhen columbie up kikis throw the clay.
>
> (87)

Still more striking is the description of Autumn.

> Syne Hervest hait, quhen Seres that goddes
> Hir barnis benit hes with abundance,
> And Bachchus god of wyne renewit hes
> Hir tome pypes in Italie and France,
> With wynis wicht and liccour of pleasaince;
> And *Copia Temporis* to fill hir horne
> That nevir wes full of quhite nor uther corne.
>
> (64–70)

This last stanza, surely, which combines the traditional Ceres and Bacchus with the first-hand precision of *tome pypes*, France, and (significantly) Italy, is very unusual for the 1480s —or any period of the Middle Ages. Even more than the opening stanzas of the *Orpheus and Eurydice* it belongs to the Renaissance, as indeed to some extent does the entire concept of a pageant of the seasons.[1] The passage is closer to Spenser's *Marriage of the Thames and Medway*,[2] than it is to anything in English medieval literature, and is thus in one sense at least profoundly original.

As a whole, the prologue is impersonal or general. The grammatical subjects of the sentences are words like 'prudence', 'God', 'Saule', 'Aristotle', and 'we'; verbs are in the third singular or first plural. 'I' as subject first appears with the main body of the fable, and remains dominant until the beginning of the *Moralitas*. The effect is twofold. Because

---

[1] *Sir Gawain and the Green Knight*, 495 ff. is perhaps the closest parallel. See also R. Tuve, *Seasons and Months* (Paris, 1933) and N. E. Enkvist, *The Seasons of the Year* (Helsingfors, 1957).

[2] *Faerie Queene*, IV. xi.

they are reported by an eye-witness, the events of the fable
acquire a particular directness and vividness. But at the same
time the construction in the first person 'places' the narrative
in a particular literary convention. Despite the fact that he
does not fall asleep, the narrator who

> movit furth betwene mid day and morne
> Unto the hege under the hawthorne grene
>
> (159–60)

sees marvels and so belongs to the literary tradition of the
dream vision; in particular, he is first cousin to the dreamer
of *Piers Plowman*. Similarity is reinforced by the line which
concludes the poet's first encounter with the birds

> So ferlyand as I had sene a farye.
>
> (154)

Compare line 6 of *Piers Plowman*—

> Me befel a ferly, of fairie me þouȝte.

For the reader, the main consequence is that symbolic or
allegorical significance is likely in the details of the landscape,
as well as in the events. Again the comparison with *Piers
Plowman* may prove helpful. In both poems the details of the
landscape are similar. Like *Piers Plowman*, the fable begins
with country workmen.

> Movand thus gait grit mirth I tuik in mynde
> Off Lauboraris to see the besynace:
> Sum makand dike, and sum the pleuch can wynd,
> Sum sawand sedis fast fra place to place,
> The harrowis hoppand in the sawaris trace.
>
> (99–103)

In Henryson, however, the figure who bears the greatest

emphasis is not the ploughman, but the sower. There is probably a double scriptural reference, on the one hand to the parable of the Sower (Matt. xiii. 3; Mark iv. 1; Luke viii. 5), on the other to that of the Tares (Matt. xiii. 24). The seed is the Word of God, but the Tares are sowed by Satan the enemy. That the latter is the reference of first importance becomes clear when the figure of the sower is identified with the fowler and his nets:

> 'Se ye yone churll', quod scho, 'beyond yond pleuch
> Fast sawand hemp, lo se, and lynget sede?
> Yone lynt will grow in lytill tyme of dede,
> And thairof will yone churll his nettis mak.'
>
> (122–5)

I have already shown the significance of the 'nettis'. The soil

> that was richt seasonable,
> Sappie, and to ressave all seidis hable
> (96–97)

has thus a fairly obvious allegorical meaning—it is the individual human soul capable of receiving wheat or tares— 'to ressave all seidis hable'. Significantly the metrical accent is on *all*. The metaphor is developed, specifically in terms of sin, in the *Moralitas* (lines 281–94).

The spring setting of the opening may be compared with the landscape amid which Eurydice meets her death in *Orpheus and Eurydice*.

> I say this be Erudices the quene,
> Quhilk walkit furth into a May morning.
> Bot with a madyn, untill a medow grene,
> To tak the air, and se the flouris spring.
>
> (92–95)

I have already commented that in Henryson the use of descriptions in this style seems always to indicate failure or worldliness of moral judgement on the part of some person in the poem. The failure on the part of the birds (other than the swallow) is clear; there may also be some implication that the failure extends to the narrator. One reason for the inclusion of the narrator may have been to provide a human centre of reference for the allegorical events of the fable—a usage which may easily be paralleled in other dream allegories.

When the lark hears the swallow's warning, she laughs—'giggled' would perhaps be a better translation.

> 'Schir swallow,' quod the Lark agane and leuch,
> 'Quhat have ye sene that causis you to drede?'
>
> (120–1)

In Henryson laughter of this kind invariably indicates moral worthlessness, temporary or permanent. Compare in *The Cock and the Fox*,

> 'Knew thou my fader?' quod the cok and leuch,
>
> (50)

and in *The Fox and the Wolf*,

> 'A silly Lowrance,' quod the wolf and leuch,
> 'It plessis me that ye ar penitent.'
>
> (71–72)

(k) *The Lion and the Mouse*—Prologue

Both Prologue and *Taill* echo other fables and the *Testament of Cresseid*. In the Prologue these echoes are mostly of *The Preaching of the Swallow*—the first stanza, for instance, might almost pass as a cento:

> In myddis of June, that Joly sweit sessoun,
> Quhen that fair Phebus with his bemis brycht
> Had dryit up the dew fra daill and doun,
> And all the land maid with his lemys lycht,
> In a morning betwix midday and nycht
> I raiss and put all slewth and sleip on syd;
> Ontill a wod I went allone but gyd.
>
> $(1–7)$

With the first line compare *Preaching of the Swallow* 155:

> We furth passit quhill June, that Jolye tyde.

The second and third lines approximately correspond to 61–63:

> And Phebus with his gowdin beames gent
> Hes purfillit and paintit plesandlie,
> With heat and mosture stilland fra the skye.

The fifth line corresponds to, and is elucidated by, 159:

> I movit furth betwene mid day and morne.

'Betwix midday and nycht' has the same meaning as 'be-twene mid day and morne', but as such a phrase seems only to occur in these two fables, and in context that from the *Prologue* is certainly the more difficult, it seems more probable than not that the Prologue deliberately echoes *The Preaching of the Swallow*.

These are mere verbal parallels, but there is also a parallel of situation. In Prologue and fable the narrator goes for a morning walk to a wood—in *The Preaching of the Swallow*,

> Unto the wod to see the flouris spring
> And heir the mavissis sing and birdis mo.
>
> $(94–95)$

The Prologue is more expansive, but the same details are emphasized:

> Sweit wes the smell of flouris quhyt and reid,
> The noyis of birdis rycht delicius . . .
>
> (8–9)

(one should not miss the sensuously effective combination of 'smell' with 'quhyt and reid').

> To heir, it was a poynt of paradyss,
> Sic myrth the maviss and the merle couth ma:
> The blosummis blyth brak up on bank and bra,
> The smell of herbis and of fowlis cry,
> Contending quha suld haif the victory.
>
> (17–21)

It has been commented that the 'first three stanzas of this fable come nearer to the conventional opening of the Chaucerian dream-allegory than Henryson approaches elsewhere'. In view of the way in which *The Preaching of the Swallow* also is closely related to dream allegory, it might be argued that the similarity of detail results from literary convention rather than direct imitation of one in the other. Only these two, however, among the *Fabillis* follow some of the conventions of dream-allegory—a fact which of itself suggests a rather close relationship. In both fables, moreover, the narrator ends his walk at a hawthorn hedge, and in both it is at the hawthorn hedge that strange happenings occur—in *The Preaching of the Swallow*

> Unto a hege under a hawthorne grene
> Off small birdis thair come a ferlye flicht—
>
> (108–9)

and in the Prologue,

> Me to conserf than fra the sonis heit,
> Undir the schaddow of an awthorne grene
> I lenyt doun amangis the flouris sweit,
> Syne maid a corss and closit baith myne ene.
>
> (22–25)

It is unusual to begin a dream-allegory under a hawthorn bush (and incidentally almost equally unusual to begin one with the sign of the cross). Henryson may mean to indicate that his allegory is something more than the usual love-vision. But whether or not this is so, the detail serves as another link between the two fables.

Aesop's reply to the dreamer's request for a fable is perhaps the most striking link of all:

> Schakand his heid, he said, 'My sone, lat be;
> For quhat is worth to tell a fenyeit taill,
> Quhen hailly preiching may no thing now availl?'
>
> (68–70)

Certainty is not possible, but it very much looks as if the final couplet refers specifically to *The Preaching of the Swallow*, to which Henryson intended that *The Lion and the Mouse* should be a sequel. The language of the Prologue would then seem to indicate that at the time of composition *The Preaching of the Swallow* had already been published and was well known. From the existence of a separate Prologue one might deduce that *The Lion and the Mouse* was published separately. No convincing explanation of the existence of the Prologue has otherwise ever been given.

The claim that Aesop studied civil law in Rome does not appear in the Bannatyne MS., which at this point seems

metrically corrupt, but appears in the Bassandyne and all
other texts, and is almost certainly to be adopted. I quote
the Bassandyne text in Harvey Wood's edition:

> My native land is Rome withoutin nay;
> And in that Towne first to the Sculis I yude,
> In Civile Law studyit full mony ane day.
>
> (1371–3)

This has sometimes been taken as an indication that Henryson
had himself studied Civil Law, possibly at Rome. I have
already indicated the probability that Henryson had legal
qualifications, and as I do not know any other author who
says that Aesop studied law at Rome, it is conceivable that
Henryson intended the description of Aesop to have some
relevance to himself. The poets of dream visions often
project aspects of themselves on to the figures of the dream,
and it is obvious that to some extent Aesop, as a projection of
Henryson, is talking, not about the *Romulus* of Gualterus
Anglicus, but about Henryson's *Morall Fabillis of Esope the
Phrygian*. At least one echo of the general Prologue might
be taken as some kind of confirmation:

> Ar ye nocht he that all thir fabillis wrate,
> Quhilk in effect, suppoiss thay fenyeit be,
> Ar full of prowdens and moralite?
>
> (59–61)

The echoes of the *Testament* are not so readily explicable.
They occur in the description of Aesop, which closely
resembles that of Mercury as god of eloquence in the planet
portraits. Mercury too is described as a poet,

> Setting sangis and singand merilie:

His Hude was reid, heklit atouir his Croun,
Lyke to ane Poeit of the auld fassoun.

(243–5)

Compare

His hude of skarlet bordourit with silk
In hekle wyss untill his girdill doun;
His bonat round wes of the auld fassoun.

(31–33)

(*l*) *The Lion and the Mouse*
(*The Taill of the Lyoun and the Mous*)

As one might expect, the relationship between *The Lion and
the Mouse* and *The Preaching of the Swallow* is close. The
latter offers a general treatment of wisdom and providence;
the former applies those ideas specifically to the Scotland of
James III, while at the same time retaining something of the
universality of *The Preaching of the Swallow*, especially in the
comic vigour of the speeches of lion and mouse. The lion, in
fact, is probably a direct and not altogether unfriendly portrait of James III—

a king with croun
Quhilk suld be walkryfe gyd and govirnour
Of his peple, and takis no laubour
To reull nor steir the land nor justice keip,
Bot lyis still in lustis, sleuth and sleip.

(255–9)

One might compare the King Humanitie of Lindsay's *Satire
of the Thrie Estaitis*.[1] The mouse represents the ordinary
people of Scotland, and while Henryson does not specifically

[1] See above, p. 121, n. 1.

say so, it is fairly clear that the hunters who trap the lion are the Scottish nobility, whose general hostility to James III is notorious. Henryson seems, in fact, to be suggesting that for James salvation from the power of the nobility depended on the equity with which his justice was administered; that so long as the commons felt no resentment against him, the nobility would be powerless to unseat him. Wisdom and providence are thus closely interconnected with justice and mercy, two words constantly repeated by the mouse.

> In every Juge mercy and reuth suld be
> As assessouris and collaterall:
> Without mercy Justice is crewelte,
> As said is in the lawis spirituall:
> Quhen rigour sittis in the tribunall,
> The equety of law quha may sustene?
> Rycht few or nane, bot mercy go betwene.
> (148–54)

Justice and mercy in turn are seen in the context of the civil and spiritual courts, from which point of view it is necessary to read the tale with the figures of *The Sheep and the Dog* in mind. Mercy finally is seen in terms of grace, a word particularly closely related both to royal and to divine power. It is by the exercise of royal grace that the lion releases the mouse, but by divine grace that the mouse is in a position to rescue the lion.

Henryson is careful to distinguish the treason of the mice from that of the hunters. The mice dance over the lion simply because he is asleep in the 'fair forest', which represents the world and its prosperity. The hunters have more positive grounds for action:

> The lyone yeid to hunt,
> For he had nocht, bot levit on his pray,
> And slew baith tame and wyld as he wes wunt,
> And in the cuntre maid a grit dirray.
>
> (190–3)

Almost certainly Henryson had in mind the repeated fifteenth-century legislation which tried to ensure that the king should 'live of his own' and so avoid burdensome impositions, which in the first place at least fell on the upper classes.[1] One of the lion's speeches may even contain a particular reference to the imprisonment of James by his noblemen after the Lauder Bridge affair in 1482:

> Quhay sall me bute? Quhay sall thir bandis breik?
> Quhay sall me put fra pane of this presoun?
>
> (220–1)

The portrait of James is not altogether unfriendly, but Henryson makes no attempt to conceal his faults—the 'lustis sleuth and sleip' of the stanza already quoted. In the words of the lion to the mouse who had pleaded mere negligence, there may even be a caricature of Stewart ideas on the divine right of kings:

> I put the caiss I had bene deid or slane,
> And syne my skin bene stoppit full of stra,
> Thocht thou had fund my figour lyand swa,
> Becaus it bair the prent of my persoun,
> Thou suld for dreid on kneis haif fallin doun.
>
> (129–33)

In the final words of Æsop, Henryson makes it finally clear

---

[1] Croft Dickinson, op. cit., pp. 290 ff.

that the primary reference of the poem is to Scotland—to
'*this* cuntre':

> Quhen this was sayid, quod Isope, 'My fair chyld,
> Persuaid the kirkmen ythandly to pray
> That tressone of this cuntre be exyld,
> And Justice ring, and lordes keip thair fey
> Unto thair soverane lord both nycht and day.'
> And with that word he vaneist and I woik,
> Syne throw the schaw my Jurney hamewart tuke.
>
> (295–301)

(m) *The Fox, the Wolf and the Husbandman*

(*The Taill of the Foxe, that begylit The Wolf, in the schadow of the Mone*)

In structure, as in symbolism, this *Taill* is unusually complex.
The assumed time of the action, for instance, is from morning to midnight, with the three principal scenes taking place
at dawn, in the evening, and in darkness by the light of the
full moon. The first and last are scenes of physical movement,
separated by an intellectual quasi-legal debate. From one
point of view, the husbandman and gadman, as labourers, are
balanced against the shiftless fox and wolf; from another, the
husbandman is opposed to the wolf with the fox as intermediary. The husbandman's house and field are opposed to
the forest haunts appropriate to the wolf.

The balance, however, is one of symbolism as well as of
narrative development. Symbolic force is most obviously
present in the night scene with which the poem closes.

Than to ane Manure place thay hyit in haist.
The nicht wes lycht, and pennyfull the Mone.
(2387–8)

In itself moonlight possesses the illusory quality which is
heightened because Henryson emphasizes, not the moon itself, but the moon's reflection in water—in his own vivid
phrase, the 'shadow' of the moon which shone in the well.
The *Moralitas* brings out at least one side of the symbolism.
The well which traps the wolf is the deceitful well of cove-
tousness with the illusory wealth of the Cabok at the foot.
Even the adjective 'pennyfull' applied to the moon is thus
significant. But it is characteristic of Henryson's generally
sardonic outlook that the wolf abandons the oxen, not even
for an illusory treasure, but for an illusory cheese. A comic
stupidity almost always forms part of his concept of the evil
man.

The opening scene of the poem is more obviously realistic,[1]
and as a consequence the reader may easily miss the symbolism, which completes the balance. The husbandman at the
plough is central. In my discussion of *The Preaching of the
Swallow* I have mentioned the allegorical significance of
labourers in Henryson's poetry (as in Langland and elsewhere).
Henryson himself emphasizes the need of such an interpretation
in the *Moralitas* of *The Fox, the Wolf and the Husbandman*:

    [1] The reader should not miss the parallel incident in Chaucer's *Friar's Tale*
(III. 1537–70) in which a summoner suggests to a fiend that he take advantage
of a carter's bad language to his horses. The fiend refuses on the ground that
'The carl spak oo thing, but he thoghte another'—a point which is relevant,
not only to the fox's allegorical role as the fiend, but also to his change of
attitude towards the husbandman. Chaucer's fiend catches the summoner in
place of the carter; Henryson's catches the wolf in place of the husbandman.

> The Husband may be callit ane godlie man,
> With quhome the Feynd falt findes (as Clerkis reids).
>
> (2434–5)

He is perhaps a little over-ingenious when he interprets the hens with which the husbandman bribes the fox, as 'warkis that fra ferme faith proceidis' (2437), but the general interpretation which he offers is closely based on qualities which in fifteenth-century terms are intrinsic to the image. The customary *Benedicite* with which the husbandman begins the day's work (as opposed to the curse into which he is momentarily forced by his wild team) may serve as confirmatory evidence. Allegorically the team has the same meaning as the 'beistis' of Aristaeus which in *Orpheus and Eurydice* represent the carnal passions, the sometimes uncontrolled appetitive power of the soul.

Henryson's treatment of the labourer resembles Langland's in at least one subsidiary point. In the Prologue to *Piers Plowman*, the ploughmen are set in immediate contrast to the proud:

> Summe putte hem to plou3, plei3ede ful selde,
> In settyng & sowyng swonke ful harde;
> Wonne þat þise wastours wiþ glotonye destroi3eth.
> And summe putte hem to pride. . . .
>
> (20–23)

So in the *Taill* the husbandman is tempted to Pride—to behave, not like a ploughman, but like a lord or king. The wolf introduces the idea:

> 'Weill' (quod the Wolff), 'I hecht the be my hand;
> Yone Carllis word, as he wer King, sall stand.'
>
> (2250–1)

When the husbandman appeals to the law, with its universal application, the wolf counters with the false conventions of an ideal of nobility like that already portrayed in *The Cock and the Fox*:

> 'Carll' (quod the Wolff), 'ane Lord, and he be leill,
> That schrinkis for schame, or doutis to be repruvit,
> His saw is ay als sickker as his Seill.'
>
> (2280–2)

It is one of the virtues of the husbandman that he is not deceived:

> I may say, and ganesay, I am na King.
> (2289)

When false ideals of nobility fail, the wolf attempts to clinch the dispute in his own favour by calling the fox as a witness—he is prepared, in other words, to fall back on a parody of legal procedure. Indeed, the whole dispute has a quasi-legal tone, and proceeds in terms of forensic rhetoric. I have already commented on the habitual use of *sententiae* in the rhetoric of persuasion. The dialogue between wolf and husbandman is in effect an exchange of *sententiae* aimed at establishing a case. At least eight are used in the four stanzas of the dispute. It is only when an impasse has been reached that both fall back on witnesses.

The *Taill* contains at least one legal quirk. In *The Sheep and the Dog*, it will be remembered, the Consistory illegally convened in the evening. When Lawrence in the present *Taill* declares, 'Now I am ane Juge amycabill' (2310), it is also evening, and in effect he is putting himself on a par with the wolf in *The Sheep and the Dog*.

In the *Moralitas* the wolf is interpreted as a wicked man who uses his power to oppress the poor. He lives in the wood of wicked riches and his social and economic position is obviously much superior to that of the poor virtuous husbandman. Such a man is particularly subject to the vicissitudes of Fortune from which the husbandman remains relatively free. From this point of view, the *Taill* retains comic overtones of the Falls of Princes tradition—overtones which become specific only as the wolf descends into the well.

> Than angerlie the Wolff upon him cryis:
> 'I cummand thus dounwart, quhy thow upwart hyis?'
> 'Schir' (quod the Foxe), 'thus fairis it off Fortoun:
> As ane cummis up, scho quheillis ane uther doun!'
>
> (2416–19)

(n) *The Fox, the Wolf and the Cadger*
(*The Taill of the Wolf that gat the Nekhering throw the wrinkis of the Foxe that begylit the Cadgear*)

The *Moralitas* of *The Fox, the Wolf and the Cadger* is Henryson's, and so likely to be of particular significance for the body of the *Taill*. The relationship is somewhat paradoxical. The cadger, the one human being of the fable, becomes Death, while, in accordance with the general Prologue—

> mony men in operatioun
> Ar lyk to beistis in thair conditioun—

it is the wolf who represents unregenerate man, and who lives 'in ane wildernes', beyond the bounds of the everyday Christian world. The *Moralitas* of *The Fox, the Wolf and the*

Husbandman offers a common medieval interpretation of the symbolism of woods which is relevant here.

> The wodds waist, quhairin wes the Wolff wyld,
> Ar wickit riches, quhilk all men gaipis to get;
> Quha traistis in sic Trusterie ar oft begyld;
> For Mammon may be callit the Devillis Net,
> Quhilk Sathanas for all sinfull hes set.
>
> (2441–5)

The fox in *The Fox, the Wolf and the Cadger* is the World, as was the lion in *The Trial of the Fox*, but the World is now seen not as king, but as the treacherous servant who plays his master false, as does Goods with Everyman. Traces, nevertheless, of the earlier regal symbolism remain. Reynard's red robe—

> 'Schir' (said the Foxe), 'ye knaw my Roib is reid,
> And thairfoir thair will na beist abyde me,
> Thocht I wald be sa fals as ffor to hyde me.'
>
> (1976–8)

may be compared with the 'rob riale' of the Lion in *The Trial of the Fox*, and there may be a punning reference to the Scots royal line in the remark of the wolf

> 'Thow[1] sall beir office, and my Stewart be.'
>
> (1966)

Finally, the herring and nekhering are 'the gold sa reid', which the world obtains for the man, and which leads to the man's final confusion.

In *The Frog and the Mouse* the paddock's ugly exterior gave warning of internal corruption. So it is here with the

---

[1] Note again the difference between 'thou' and 'ye'. (See above, p. 135, n. 1 and p. 136, n. 1.)

fox—shape, colour, scent, and physical peculiarities give warning of his evil nature—

> My tippit twa eiris, and my twa gray Ene,
> Garris me be kend, quhair I wes never sene.
> (1991–2)

But the reactions of the wolf are different from those of the mouse, who was persuaded to trust the paddock only against her better judgement. In the present fable the fox again and again hints to the wolf of the danger he is running, but the wolf is blind and does not recognize the warning.

> 'Schir' (said the Foxe) 'that beist ye mycht call blind,
> That micht not eschaip than ffra me ane myle.'
> (1988–9)

Henryson's irony is seen when the wolf uses a proverb— 'Falset will failye ay at the latter end' (1997)—that is later to recoil on his own head, when he is physically blinded by the cadger.

> He mycht not se, he wes sa verray blind,
> Nor wit reddilie quhether it wes nicht or day.
> (2184–5)

Such irony indeed is a recurrent feature of the *Taill*. The fox tells the wolf that if he follows the advice given to him, he will certainly get the nekhering (2131–2). He advises him to lay his head on a hard place (2137), and that if he gets the nekhering he will not need to look for fish again until after Easter (2152–3). He crosses the wolf and tells him

> 'Wend quhen ye will, I dar be warrand now
> That ye sall de na *suddan* deith this day.'
> (2156–7)

The metrical emphasis falls beautifully on 'suddan'. And of
course there is the irony of the song, 'huntis up, up, upon hie'
(2083), sung by the cadger when the fox is already rifling his
creels.

Two worlds of religion meet in the *Taill*. Both fox and
wolf pay lip-service to the Christian year:

> 'Schir', said the Foxe, 'it is Lentring, ye se;
> I can nocht fische, ffor weiting off my feit.'
> (2000–1)

The relevance of the herring thus becomes clear—

> 'Thairfoir I reid that we se ffor sum wayis
> To get sum fische aganis thir fasting dayis'
> (2033–4)

or later

> 'Now, suithlie, Schir, micht we that hering fang,
> It wald be fische to us thir fourtie dayis.'
> (2119–20)

On the other hand, the fox swears loyalty to the wolf in quite
different terms.

> 'Be Juppiter, and on pane off my heid,
> I sall be trew to you, quhill I be deid.'
> (2026–7)

The only other character in the *Fabillis* to swear by Jupiter
is the paddock of *The Frog and the Mouse*, who falsely promises to convey the mouse to the other side of the river.

> Scho golkit up and to the hevin can cry,
> 'Thou Jupiter, of natur god and king,
> I mak ane aith to the trewly that I
> This littil mouss sall our the wattir bring.'
> (92–95)

The World, that is to say, and the Flesh (the paddock) pay
lip-service to God, but when man's soul is at stake, as it is in
both fables, it is Jupiter, the god of Nature, by whom they
swear, with an intention not unlike that of Edmund in *King
Lear*:

> Thou, Nature, art my goddess; to thy law
> My services are bound. Wherefore should I
> Stand in the plague of custom?
>
> (I. ii. 1–3)

The World is associated with the Devil as well as the Flesh,
and it is by the cadger that this last association is made plain.
To his cost he assumed that the Devil was dead.

> 'Heir lyis the Devyll' (quod he) 'deid in ane dyke.'
>
> (2062)

The spoken word occupies an unusual proportion of the
Taill—not the formal exchange of speeches, but rapid dialogue, in which fox and wolf have each only a few lines. Each,
for instance, speaks twice in the following stanza.

> 'Bot quhat wes yone the Carll cryit on hie,
> And schuke his hand,' quod he, 'hes thou no feill?'
> 'Schir' (said the Foxe), 'that I can tell trewlie;
> He said the Nekhering wes in till the creill.'
> 'Kennis thow that hering?' 'Ye, Schir, I ken it weill,
> And at the creill mouth I had it thryis but doubt;
> The wecht off it neir tit my tuskis out.'
>
> (2112–18)

Correspondingly throughout, whether the speaker is cadger,
wolf, or fox, the stylistic level is colloquial, as, for instance,
when the cadger sees the apparently dead fox.

> 'Thair sall na Pedder, for purs, nor yit for gluifis,
> Nor yit ffor poyntis pyke your pellet ffra me;
> I sall off it mak mittennis to my lufis,
> Till hald my handis hait quhair ever I be;
> Till Flanderis sall it never saill the se.'
>
> (2070–4)

Pedder, purs, gluifis, poyntis, pyke, pellet, mittennis, lufis, even in this context *hait,* are all words appropriate to low style, and in this respect the lines are typical of the whole fable. The only feature which might suggest a different aim is the unusual number of proverbs introduced. I have already quoted 'Falset will failye ay at the latter end' (1997), and there are at least ten others. In the Middle Ages, as earlier and later, proverbs, *sententiae* were considered an ornament of style. This is not, however, to say that *sententiae* were appropriate only to high style; stylistic level was determined by the *sententia* itself, and by the manner of expression. The proverbs used in the *Taill* are appropriate to low style, and generally express a distinctly worldly and opportunistic philosophy, like that of Polonius in *Hamlet* or Ulysses in *Troilus and Cressida*:

> he is ane fule perfay
> That with his maister fallis in ressoning
>
> (2014–15)

or

> For he that will not laubour and help him selff,
> In to thir dayis, he is not worth ane fle.
>
> (2044–5)

or

> Ane wicht man wantit never, and he wer wyis.
>
> (2108)

Appropriately, most are put in the month of the worldly fox;

but, as opposed to this, when the wolf does use *sententiae*, the effect is to prove his blindness, not his worldly wisdom. The cadger too is mistaken in his one *sententia*.

> 'Heir lyis the Devyll' (quod he), 'deid in ane dyke.
> (2063)

The proverb ran 'Seldome lyes the divel dead by ane dycksyd'.

Two minor points may be added. The senses emphasized in the fable are the lower—smell and taste. Other animals recognize the fox by his smell—'Ane lang space ffra thame thay will feill my sent' (1983). The smell of the herring attracts the fox—'The Foxe the flewer off the fresche hering feillis' (2030). And although the apparent reference is to sight, the description of the nekhering given by the fox is calculated to make the wolf's mouth water:

> It is ane syde off Salmond, as it wair,
> And callour, pypand lyke ane Pertrik Ee;
> It is worth all the hering ye have thair.
> (2126–8)

The sensual emphasis, that is to say, corresponds to the worldliness and low motives of the characters, the fox in particular.

The second point is somewhat more abstract. In the fox, the wolf, and the cadger it is easy enough to see the World, Man, and Death. That the herring, which represents Gold, should be the property of Death, is less obvious. Two possible explanations suggest themselves. In the first place, fable and *Moralitas* do not often absolutely correspond—*The Frog and the Mouse*, in which almost every detail bears an allegorical significance, is not typical. At this point, in other words, the correspondence may simply break down. But Chaucer's

Pardoner's Tale illustrates another possibility. There the three revellers set out to kill Death. They are told that they will find him under a tree, but instead they find gold, which nevertheless causes their death. Gold belongs to Death, and they are linked in terms of the text *Radix malorum est cupiditas*, the application of which to Henryson's fable is so close and obvious that it can scarcely be accidental.

(o) *The Wolf and the Wether*
(*The Taill of the Wolf and the Wedder*)

The landscape of the tale—the shepherd with his fold near a forest—carries immediate allegorical conviction—the state or church under a good ruler with the forces of evil lurking in the immediate neighbourhood. The other fables provide no other landscape exactly parallel, but one may compare the interpretation of the wood in *The Fox, the Wolf, and the Husbandman*:

> The wodds waist, quhairin wes the Wolff wyld,
> Ar wickit riches, quhilk all men gaipis to get.
>
> (2441–2)

Compare too the 'wildernes' of *The Fox, the Wolf and the Cadger* and the 'thornie schaw' of *The Cock and the Fox*— both homes of evil-doers.

It would nevertheless be unsatisfactory to make the landscape the sole basis of interpretation. In the first place, Henryson in the *Moralitas* lays greatest emphasis on the figure of the sheep disguised as a dog, which he interprets as a poor man made presumptuous by riches of array, and so coming to a bad end. I have already shown that Henryson sometimes reserves the particular rather than the general application of a fable for the *Moralitas*: he may here be following the same pattern—he may indeed intend a reference to a particular poor man, that Robert Cochrane, say, who in 1482 was hanged on Lauder Bridge:

> Thay think thay hald of nane, be thay als gay,
> Bot counterfute ane Lord in all degre
> Out of thair cais in pryde thay clym sa hie
> That thay forbeir thair better in na steid,
> Quhill sum man tit thair heillis over thair heid.
>
> (2597–601)

I should not, however, like to forward such an interpretation as any more than a probability.

The second point is that the sequence of events, like the style generally, remains consistently beneath the level appropriate to allegory as opposed to satire. Henryson is, of course, too good a poet to maintain a single level throughout the poem, but in this *Taill* his few gestures towards high style are more than usually obvious as burlesque. There is, for instance, the shepherd's lament for his dead dog:

> It wald have maid ane mannis hart sair to se
> The selie scheiphirdis lamentatioun:
> 'Now is my Darling deid, allace' (quod he)—
>
> (2469–71)

or the sheep's heroically alliterative pursuit of the wolf:

> Went never Hound mair haistelie fra the hand,
> Quhen he wes rynnand maist raklie at the Ra.
>
> (2518–19)

Such instances apart, the most obvious stylistic features of the *Taill* are those. In the first place, it tends to the mono-syllabic:

> To brek your hart ffor baill it is na bute;
> For ane deid Dogge ye na cair on yow kyith.
> Ga ffeche him hither, and fla his skyn off swyth.
>
> (2478–80)

Every word but one in these lines is a monosyllable. The second is negative—Henryson's characteristic rhyming on words of Latin origin scarcely occurs in the *Taill*, but is reserved for the first stanza of the *Moralitas*—one of the most Lydgatean stanzas he ever wrote:

> Esope, that poete, first Father of this Fabill,
> Wrait this Parabole, quhilk is convenient,
> Because the sentence wes fructuous and agreabill.
> In Moralitie exemplative prudent,
> Quhais problemes bene verray excellent
> Throw similitude of figuris, to this day
> Gevis doctrine to the Redaris of it ay.
>
> (2588–94)

Third is the occurrence of a number of slightly clumsy feminine rhymes, usually in the closing couplet of a stanza, and usually with an effect of burlesque:

> The Wolff ran still quhill ane strand stude behind him,
> Bot ay the neirar the Wedder he couth bind him.
>
> (2537–8)

Last is the occurrence of a number of *sententiae* pitched at a deliberately low level:

> Quha sayis ane scheip is daft, thay lieit of it.
>
> (2492)

> Ane flear gettis ane follower commounly.
>
> (2576)

Ane full gude servand will crab his Maister anis.

(2580)

All these are elements of low style, and correspondingly the plot turns on two *fabliau*-like incidents—the dog's skin stitched over the sheep, and the flight of the wolf who fouls the ground in his terror.

It follows that none of the reader's sympathy should be wasted on the sheep—if his sympathy is directed anywhere, it is rather to the deceived wolf. The effect of the *Taill* is to reverse the shepherd's judgement:

Quha sayis ane scheip is daft, thay lieit of it.

(2492)

The sheep is introduced in uncomplimentary terms:

With that ane Wedder wrechitlie wan on fute

(2476)

and his proposal that the shepherd should clothe him in the dog's skin is self-evident farce. His false pride is emphasized:

Than worth the Wedder wantoun off his weid:
'Now off the Wolff' (quod he) 'I have na dreid.'

(2495–6)

His courage is in appearance only:

He wes mekill and *semit* to be stout.

(2508)

So also he is given, but deliberately ignores, the chance to rescue the lamb, while at the same time honourably disengaging himself from his useless pursuit. The transformation that follows is partly physical:

ane breir busk raif rudelie off the skyn.

(2545)

More striking however is the transformation of the sheep's
language from the heroic to the humble before he is killed by
the wolf:

> 'For quhat enchessoun this Doggis skyn have ye borne?'
> 'Maister' (quod he), 'bot to have playit with yow;
> I yow requyre that ye nane uther trow.'
>
> (2557–9)

The effect of comic but deserved humiliation is central to
Henryson's intention in the poem.

APPENDIX I

The Text of the *Morall Fabillis*

THE *Fabillis* were probably written between 1475 and 1490, but the most important manuscripts and printed editions all date from a period almost a century later. The Bannatyne MS. is dated 1568, although for the collection of items an earlier date is probable. Harleian MS. 3865 is dated 1571. The date of the Charteris printed text is 1570, and that of the Bassandyne 1571. Of less importance because very incomplete are the Makculloch MS., which contains a text of the general Prologue and *The Cock and the Jewel*, and the Asloan MS., which contains a text of *The Two Mice*. The versions in both manuscripts probably belong to the early sixteenth century. The practice of editors in dealing with these authorities has varied. Laing (1865) produced a composite text; his choice of reading was based only on personal preference or intuition. Diebler (1886) produced an edition of Harleian MS. 3865. Gregory Smith (1906) printed all the texts available to him. Harvey Wood (1933 and 1958) based his edition on the newly rediscovered Bassandyne print, as did Charles Elliott (1963).[1] None of the editors advanced any real textual argument to justify the procedure which he had adopted.

The central textual problem is fourfold. (i) For the greater part of the text, the Bannatyne MS. is the oldest extant version. On the other hand, (ii) the order of the *Fabillis* in Bannatyne differs strikingly from that of the other authorities, (iii) only ten of the

[1] D. Laing, *Poems and Fables of Robert Henryson* (Edinburgh, 1865); A. R. Diebler, 'Henrisone's Fabeldichtungen', *Anglia*, ix (1886), pp. 337 ff.; G. Gregory Smith, *Poems of Robert Henryson*, 3 vols., S.T.S. (Edinburgh, 1906–14); H. Harvey Wood, *Poems and Fables of Robert Henryson* (Edinburgh, 1933, 1958); C. Elliott, *Robert Henryson. Poems* (Oxford, 1963). For the Bassandyne text, I have used Harvey Wood; for Bannatyne, W. Tod Ritchie, *The Bannatyne Manuscript*, iv, S.T.S. (Edinburgh, 1930).

thirteen extant *Fabillis* are preserved in Bannatyne, and in those some stanzas appear to be missing, and (iv) Bannatyne was a careless copyist.

(i) is a slight indication that Bannatyne should form the basis of a text, a proposal which would seem to be counterbalanced by the other three observations. My purpose in this section is, first, to show that (ii) and (iii) are less important than they might at first appear, and second, to show that in general Bannatyne's text is so much superior to any of the others that it must necessarily form the basis of a satisfactory edition.

First, then, there is no real evidence that Henryson had finally decided on an order for the complete set of *Fabillis*. One sequence, *The Cock and the Fox*, *The Fox and the Wolf*, *The Trial of the Fox*, is established as Henryson's by internal evidence. The sequence is preserved in Bannatyne as elsewhere. For the rest, the existence of two Prologues may be regarded as particularly significant. Of those, in most texts one serves to introduce the *Fabillis* as a whole, but in Bannatyne and Makculloch only *The Cock and the Jewel*. The other is a Prologue to *The Lion and the Mouse*. In the first, the difference between Bannatyne, Makculloch, and the other texts has not hitherto received enough attention. In Bassandyne, for instance, the Prologue is made general by the single word 'fabillis'.

> My Author in his Fabillis tellis how
> That brutal beistis spak, and Understude,
> In to gude purpois dispute, and argow,
> Ane Sillogisme propone, and eik conclude.
>
> (43–46)

Bannatyne (like Makculloch) has 'fable' in the singular, and in other respects his text seems better:

> Myne auctour in his fable tellis fow (*leg.* how)
> That brutall beistis spak and undirstud,
> And till gud purpoiss dispit and argow,
> A sylogysme propone and eik exclud.
>
> (43–46)

In particular, Bannatyne's 'exclud' (used of an excluded middle?) may seem more probable, because more difficult and more pointed, than the comparatively obvious 'conclude' of Bassandyne.

Against this argument one might advance another based on source material. One of Henryson's sources was the Latin verse-*Romulus*, together with a derivative French *Isopet*.[1] In these, the first fable is *The Cock and the Jewel*, which is preceded by a general Prologue not unrelated to Henryson's. The relationship between Henryson's Prologue, it might be argued, and that of the Latin and French, indicates that from the beginning Henryson intended his own as a Prologue to the entire series. Two points, however, still require consideration. If the Bannatyne reading is accepted, Henryson may have meant his Prologue to be both general and particular to *The Cock and the Jewel*—he may, in other words, at one time have intended to write individual prologues to each of the *Fabillis*. In the second place, it is worth considering the group of fables for which Henryson may have intended to supply a general Prologue. As I hope to prove in later appendixes, the *Fabillis* draw on five main sources:

(a) The Latin verse-*Romulus* of Gualterus Anglicus (? c. 1175), and its derivative, the thirteenth-century French *Isopet de Lyon*.

(b) Chaucer's *Nun's Priest's Tale*.

(c) Caxton's *History of Reynard the Fox* (1481).

(d) The *Roman de Renart*.

(e) Caxton's *Aesop* (1484).

It seems probable that, at least in the first place, Henryson's general Prologue, related as it is to the general Prologue to the verse-*Romulus* and the *Isopet de Lyon*, should have been intended to introduce the fables based on these same sources. These are in the order in which they appear in the Latin, *The Cock and the Jewel* (1),

[1] For Henryson's sources, see appendixes II and III. *The Wolf and the Wether* is based on Caxton's 'The Dogge, the Wulf and the Whether' (*The Fables of Aesop*, ed. J. Jacobs, London, 1899, pp. 180–2).

The Wolf and the Lamb (II), *The Frog and the Mouse* (III), *The Sheep and the Dog* (IV), *The Two Mice* (XII), *The Lion and the Mouse* (XVIII), and *The Preaching of the Swallow* (XXV). The order of Bassandyne is almost completely different, and fables derived from other sources are intruded into the series. In Bannatyne, however, *The Cock and the Jewel* is followed by *The Frog and the Mouse* (III), *The Two Mice* (XII), *The Sheep and the Dog* (IV), *The Wolf and the Lamb* (II) and *The Lion and the Mouse* (XVIII), with which, so far as the *Fabillis* are concerned, the manuscript ends. *The Preaching of the Swallow* (XXV) is the first of the *Fabillis* anthologized by Bannatyne, and Henryson's treatment of it, particularly the long, directly philosophical and theological introduction, serves to distinguish it from the others. It should also be noted that Henryson specifically mentions Aesop as his source only in *The Cock and the Jewel, The Frog and the Mouse, The Two Mice, The Sheep and the Dog, The Lion and the Mouse, The Preaching of the Swallow, The Fox, the Wolf and the Husbandman*, and *The Wolf and the Wether*.

One other point should be added. The *Moralitas* to *The Sheep and the Dog* contains the following lines:

> Off this fals tod becauss I spak befoir,
> And of this gled quhat thay mycht signify,
> Off thair natur as now I speik no moir.
> (Bannatyne, 134–6)

These lines surely imply that Henryson had previously set out the *significatio* not only of the toad, but also of the gled—in other words, that *The Frog and the Mouse* as well as *The Cock and the Fox* and *The Trial of the Fox* should precede *The Sheep and the Dog*. Such an arrangement is only found in Bannatyne.

In this way it is possible to show some significance in the order of Bannatyne, a significance which in the other authorities is lost.

The omissions in Bannatyne are open to a similar interpretation. Bannatyne omits *The Fox, the Wolf and the Cadger, The Fox, the Wolf and the Husbandman* and *The Wolf and the Wether*, three fables which elsewhere occur as a group. The fact most significant here is that *The Fox, the Wolf and the Husbandman* and *The Wolf and the Wether* have a common source in Caxton's *Aesop* (1484). No other among the *Fabillis* is based on this work. *The Fox, the Wolf and the Cadger* is based directly on the *Roman de Renart*. Again, no other fable has the same source. Because they belong most directly to the Aesopic tradition, and set the form for the collection as a whole, one may plausibly assume that the group already mentioned, based on the verse-*Romulus* and the *Isopet de Lyon*, represents the first of the *Fabillis* to be composed. Two other groups are related to significantly dated works: *The Fox and the Wolf* and *The Trial of the Fox* to Caxton's History of *Reynard the Fox* (1481), and those based on Caxton's *Aesop* (1484). *The Cock and the Fox*, based on Chaucer's *Nun's Priest's Tale*, is so closely related to *The Fox and the Wolf* and *The Trial of the Fox* that its composition must have preceded, or been simultaneous with, that of the other two. There is thus no reason against the assumption that all the *Fabillis*, save the group omitted in Bannatyne, were composed before, say, 1482 or 1483. Two at least of the fables omitted, however, must have been composed in or after 1484. I suggest that all three belong to a later period, and that Bannatyne's source was, or was derived from, an early version of the *Fabillis* which did not include the additions made after 1485.

It remains to establish the verbal superiority of Bannatyne. The relative authority of variant readings may be tentatively established by sense, metre, and such principles as *difficilior lectio*, haplography, and dittography. An author's stylistic habits may be of textual importance, as on occasions may the historical period at which his work was copied or printed. I subjoin a highly selective group of examples which suggest the superiority of the Bannatyne text.

(*a*) *Sense.* Many of the corruptions discussed later are first indicated by a meaningless reading in Bassandyne (to which I shall refer as the normally accepted text). Here only one needs specific examination. In the *Moralitas* to the *Trial of the Fox* Bassandyne reads:

> The Meir is Men of gude conditioun,
> As Pilgrymes Walkand in this wildernes,
> Approvand that for richt Religioun
> Thair God onlie to pleis in everilk place.
>
> (1111–14)

In the context of fable and *Moralitas* 'Men of gude conditioun' does not seem appropriate or meaningful. I cannot make any coherent sense of 1113. Bannatyne is superior on both counts, and at the same time contains in itself an explanation of the corruption or deliberate alteration in Bassandyne's text, printed as it was in post-Reformation Scotland.

> This mere is men of contemplatioun
> Off pennance walkand in this wildernace
> As monkis and othir men of religioun
> That presis God to pleiss in every place.
>
> (302–5)

(*b*) *Metre*. In *The Fox and the Wolf* Bassandyne reads:

> Quhill that the Goddes off the flude
> Phebus had callit to the harbery.
>
> (621–2)

Bannatyne preserves a convincing and metrically superior reading, which indicates haplography as the source of corruption:

> Quhill that Thetes, the goddess of the flude.
>
> (8)

In *The Two Mice* Bassandyne reads:

> In stubbill array throw gers and corne.
>
> (253)

Bannatyne reads:

> In skugry ay throw rankest girss and corne.
>
> (92)

Elliott[1] has defended 'In stubbill array' but the difficult and dialectal

---

[1] Op. cit., p. 133.

'In skugry ay' (= 'always stealthily') would easily be corrupted to the more Anglified 'In stubbill array'. The omission of 'rankest' is perhaps the result of haplography with 'array'.

(*c*) *Difficilior lectio.* This has already been illustrated. I subjoin four additional examples.

(i) In *The Fox and the Wolf* Bassandyne reads:

> And speik we off the subtell aventure
> And destenie that to this Foxe befell,
> Quhilk durst na mair with waitting Intermell.
>
> (616–18)

Bannatyne reads the less usual (and more vivid) 'miching' for 'waitting'. The alliteration of 'miching' with 'Intermell' is typically Henrysonian.

Bannatyne also reads 'fatal' for the 'subtell' of Bassandyne. Sense, and the alliteration of 'fatal' with 'fox' suggest that here too Bannatyne preserves the better reading. 'Subtell' may result from 'f' being read as long 's'.

(ii) In *The Cock and the Fox* Bassandyne reads the metrically deficient

> 'How, murther, hay!' with ane hiddeous beir.
>
> (486)

The Bannatyne reading improves the metre:

> 'How, murthour, reylock!' with a hiddeous beir.
>
> (90)

Professor Bruce Dickins[1] has pointed out that the difficult 'reylock' is probably a derivative of OE. *rēaflāc*, 'robbery', which survived into the fifteenth century as a technical term (*reyflake, revelayk*) in Scots legal usage.

(iii) Later in *The Cock and the Fox* Bassandyne reads:

> 'He had' (quod scho) 'kittokis ma than sevin'.
>
> (533)

---

[1] *T.L.S.*, 21 February 1924.

Bannatyne reads:

> Seiss coud he nocht with sissokkis mo than sevin.
>
> (137)

'Sissokkis' (diminutive of Cis from Cecily) is the more difficult, and as meaningful, the preferable reading. Compare 'Cesse the souteresse' in *Piers Plowman* B, v. 315. The argument is strengthened by the alliteration in Bannatyne as compared to Bassandyne.

(iv) In *The Frog and the Mouse* Bassandyne reads:

> With all hir mycht scho forsit hir to swym.
>
> (2887)

Bannatyne reads:

> Scho bowtit up and foirsit hir to swyme.
>
> (111)

The dialectal 'bowtit up' (= 'bobbed up') is clearly better and more difficult than the colourless 'With all hir mycht'. Compare also in the *Two Mice* Bannatyne's

> In steid of spyce to cresch thair teithis withall
>
> (126)

with Bassandyne's

> In steid of spyce to gust thair mouth withall.
>
> (287)

(*d*) *Haplography* has already been illustrated. A double instance of dittography is to be found in *The Fox and the Wolf*. Bassandyne reads:

> My destenie, and eik my weird I ken,
> My aventure is cleirlie to me kend;
> With mischeif myngit is my mortall men,
> My misleving the soner bot gif I men.
>
> (649–52)

The most immediate sign of corruption here is the meaningless 'men' of 651. Bannatyne preserves the much better

> My destany and eik my werd I watt
> Myn evintour is cleirly to me kend

With mischeif mynyet is my mortall fait
My mysleving the soner bot I men.

(36–39)

Here 'watt' is synonymous with the 'ken' of Bassandyne. Under the influence of 'kend' in the second line, the scribe or compositor unconsciously substituted 'ken' for 'watt' in the first line, and it then proved necessary to change 'fait' in order to preserve the rhyme. The process was probably conscious, but may have been unconscious.

(*e*) Of themselves, those textual comparisons would establish the general superiority of Bannatyne. More striking, and even more decisive, however, are a group of readings whose presence in Bannatyne, but absence in other authorities, is to be explained in terms of the political and religious circumstances of post-Reformation Scotland. One such, from the *Moralitas* to *The Trial of the Fox*, has already been quoted. Even more striking is another stanza from the same Moralitas. In Bannatyne this originally read:

O Mary myld, medeator of mercy meke,
Sitt doun before thy Sone celestiall:
For us synnaris his celsitude beseke.

(330–2)

Bannatyne himself substituted the more Protestant:

O Lord eternall, medeator for us mast meke,
Sit doun before thy Fader celestiall.

Bassandyne reads:

O Mediatour! mercifull and meik,
Thow soveraigne Lord, and King Celestiall,
Thy celsitude maist humillie we beseik.

(1139–41)

There can be no doubt that Bannatyne's first version is nearest to what Henryson actually wrote. Compare too the first stanza of the *Moralitas* to *The Fox and the Wolf*. Bassandyne reads:

> This suddand deith, and unprovysit end
> Of this fals Tod, without provision,
> Exempill is exhortand folk to amend,
> For dreid of sic ane lyke confusion;
> For mony now hes gude professioun,
> Yit not repentis, nor for thair sinnis greit,
> Because thay think thair lustie lyfe sa sweit.
>
> (775–81)

The meaningless 'provision' and 'hes gude professioun' already suggest corruption in the text. Bannatyne has the obviously better

> This suddane deid and unprouisit end
> Off this fals tod without contritioun,
> Exemple is exhortand folk to mend
> For dreid of sic a lyke conclusioun:
> For monye gois now to confessioun
> Can nocht repent, nor for thair synnis greit,
> Becaus thai think thair lustye lyfe so sweit.
>
> (162–8)

In the Prologue to *The Lion and the Mouse*, Bassandyne reads:

> I lenit doun amang the flouris sweit,
> Syne cled my heid, and closit baith my ene.
>
> (1344–5)

Bannatyne has the obviously better

> Syne maid a corss, and closit baith myne ene.
>
> (25)

The last example is in some ways the most instructive of all, as showing the extreme detail to which the ecclesiastical censors were prepared to work. In the *Moralitas* to *The Frog and the Mouse* Bassandyne reads:

> My freind, thairfoir, mak the ane strang Castell
> Of Faith in Christ.
>
> (2966–7)

Bannatyne reads:

> My freind thairfoir mak the a strang castell
> Of gud deidis.
>
> (190–1)

Calvinist views on Justification by Faith alone have clearly guided the reviser.

The general conclusion must, I think, be that Bannatyne offers the only satisfactory basis for the text of ten of the *Fabillis*. For the others Bassandyne may be used, but only with extreme caution. In the preceding chapters I have used a text based on Bannatyne wherever such a proceeding was possible.

APPENDIX II

The *Morall Fabillis* and the Aesopic Tradition

THE twelfth-century verse-*Romulus* sometimes attributed to Gualterus Anglicus, archbishop of Palermo and chaplain to Henry II of England, a work which has generally been recognized as a primary source for the *Morall Fabillis*, is in four manuscripts accompanied by a thirteenth-century translation and expansion into French verse. Three of these contain the translation which has come to be known as the *Isopet I*; one contains the *Isopet de Lyon*.[1] Several factors combine to suggest that when Henryson began work on the *Fabillis*, he had in his possession, or at least was familiar with, a manuscript or printed edition of this kind. The evidence is best illustrated in terms of the general *Prologue* and three fables, *The Cock and the Jasp*, *The Sheep and the Dog*, and *The Two Mice*.

In line 28 of Henryson's Prologue, *Dulcius arrident seria picta*

---

[1] These works are most conveniently consulted in J. Bastin, *Recueil généra des Isopets*, Vol. II (Paris, Société des Anciens Textes Français, 1930), which contains an Introduction, a text of the *Romulus* of Gualterus and the *Avianus*, and texts of *Isopet de Lyon*, *Isopet I*, and the unimportant *Isopet III*. All my references are to this edition. Cf. also L. Hervieux, *Les Fabulistes latins* (2nd edit., Paris, 1893), 5 volumes, and the useful introduction to the first volume of Bastin's *Recueil* (Paris, 1929). In the present chapter I have confined myself to the sources and possible sources which seem of greatest historical and literary importance. Henryson, for example, may have known Lydgate's early *Isopes fabules* (H. N. MacCracken, *Minor Poems*, II. 566 ff.) but, as Schirmer remarks, 'there is little that is praiseworthy in these 959 lines'. (*John Lydgate. A Study in the Culture of the XVth Century*, translated by Ann E. Keep, London, 1961, p. 23.) Compare also I. A. W. Jamieson, *The Poetry of Robert Henryson: a Study of the Uses of Source Material* (unpublished Ph.D. Thesis in the library of the University of Edinburgh). See too Appendix I, p. 191, note 1.

Iocis is a direct quotation of the second line of Gualterus' prologue. Elsewhere, however, sense and also rhyme seems to echo the prologues of the French versions.

> Thir nutis schellis, thocht thai be hard and tuich,
> Thay hald the cirnall, sweit and delectable;
> So lyis thair a doctryne wyse anewch
> And full of fruct undir a fenyeit fable.
> As clerkis sayis, it is rycht proffitable.
>
> (15–19)

To this corresponds in the *Moralitas* to Gualterus's Prologue

> Ut nucleum celat arida testa bonum.
> (12)

The rhyme *delectable*, *fable*, *proffitable*, however, recurs in the French of *Isopet I.*

> Ce livret que cy vous recite
> Plaist a ouir et si profite;
> Et pour ce que plus delitables
> Soit, y a maintes beles fables.
>
> (1–4)

> Fleur, que a oïr est delitables,
> Fruis, quar en fait est profitables.
> (11–12)

In this particular instance, the *Isopet de Lyon* offers a resemblance somewhat less striking, but, in that the words *delitauble*, *fauble*, and *profitauble* are present in that order, still complete:

> Li fruiz est bons, la flours novele,
> Delitauble, plaisanz et bele.
> Li flours est example de fauble,
> Li fruiz doctrine profitauble.
>
> (11–14)

The *Isopet de Lyon* too is closer to Henryson in other matters of diction. With

So springis thair a morall sweit sentence
Out of the scitell dyt of poetre

(12–13)

compare

Silz livres qu'est ci en presence
Contient de grant profit sentence.
Raisons qu'est de solez paree
Est plus voluntiers escoutee,
Car cilz fait comm' un soutilz laz,
Qui melle sent avuec soulez.

(1–6)

It should be noted that in the Latin there is no cognate of *delectable*, *profittable*, *sentence*, or *scitell*.

The title of Henryson's first *Taill*, *The Cock and the Jasp*, is closely paralleled by *Isopet de Lyon*, *Dou Poul et de la Jaspe*. In *Isopet I* it is *Du Coc et de l'Esmeraude*; in Gualterus, *De Gallo et Iaspide*. Henryson, in other words, is slightly closer to *Isopet de Lyon* than to Gualterus. So in the remainder of the *Taill* the *Isopet de Lyon* sometimes offers closer parallels than either Gualterus or *Isopet I*. For example,

It is pety I suld the fynd, for quhy
Thy grit vertew nor yit thy cullour cleir
I may nowther extoll nor magnify,
And thou to me ma mak bot littill cheir;
To grit lordis thocht thou be leif and deir,
I lawfe fer bettir thing of less availl,
As cafe or corne to fill my tome entrell.

(85–91)

Compare

Las! ta bontey ne ta valour
Ne me fait ne froit ne chalour.
Estrange est a moi ta nature,
En toi ne truis point de pasture.

> Muez ainz grains de fromant ou d'orge,
> Quar miez me font ovrir la gorge.
>
> (I. 17–22)

To this in the Latin corresponds *plus amo cara minus* (I. 8), which approximates closely only to 'I lawfe fer bettir thing of less availl'. There is nothing to correspond in *Isopet I*.

Isopet de Lyon is also uniquely close to Henryson in one line of the *Moralitas*. Henryson, who has interpreted the jasp as 'perfyt prudens and cunnyng', adds

> Bot now, allaiss, this Jasp is tynt and hid
>
> (155)

With this compare and contrast

> Sapience qu'est espandue
> Entre Fous, c'est chose perdue.
>
> (I. 29–30)

Here *perdue* corresponds to 'tynt'. But there is also a suggestion of the scriptural pearls before swine (Matthew vii. 6), which Henryson may have made more specific in his reference to the sow,

> to quhome men for the nons
> In hir drafe troch wald saw the pretius stons.
>
> (145–6)

In *The Sheep and the Dog*, the most striking parallel is to be found in the description of the legal officers of the court. In Henryson, the wolf is judge, the fox clerk; the kite and vulture are the dog's advocates:

> The fox wes clerk And notar in that causs:
> The gled, the grip up at the bar couth stand
> As advocatis expert in to the lawis.
>
> (29–31)

In Gualterus, as in *Isopet I*, the judge is not identified; the dog's advocates are the kite, the fox and the wolf:

> Pro cane stat Milvus, stat Vulpes, stat Lupus.
>
> (IV. 3.)

In *Isopet de Lyon*, the fox is not mentioned, but the wolf is judge, and the dog's advocates are the kite and the vulture:

> En cel plait est juges li Lous:
> Cilz juges est mout perillous.
> Li Chiens avoit bons consoillours,
> (Por son plait ne querez moillours),
> Lo Nieble et lo Voutour ensamble.
>
> (IV. 3–7)

The details in Henryson, that is to say, are identical with those in *Isopet de Lyon*, save for the presence of the fox, which we may perhaps assume to have been derived from the Latin of Gualterus.

The most striking resemblances to the *Isopets*, however, are to be found in the series of fables dealing with mice, and in particular *The Two Mice*. Henryson's mice, for instance, are almost invariably feminine, a gender for which the Latin text offers no authority. But the usual French word for mouse, *souris*, is feminine, and when the author of *Isopet de Lyon* uses the alternative, *rate*, he too chooses a feminine form. His title for *The Two Mice* is *De la Rate privee et de la savaige; Isopet I* has *De la Souris de bonne vile et de vilaige*. The French of both has *sœur* to correspond to Henryson's 'sister' in this as in the other fables:

> 'My fair sistir', quod scho, 'haif me excusit;
> This rude dyet and I can nocht accord.'
>
> (57–58)

Correspondingly in *Isopet I* we have such examples as

> Plus ain mes feves, douce suer,
> Asseur et a pais de mon cuer,
> Que de viandes habundance.
>
> (XII. 61–63)

or in *Isopet de Lyon*,

> Suer, mout me plait ta charitey;
> Vien avuec moi en ma citey.
> Tu moinnes cy mout povre vie;
> Ma maison est mout bien garnie:

> Il n'est riens, puis que il te plaise,
> Que tu n'i trovoies a t'aise.
>
> (XII. 37–42)

It should be added that this last quotation parallels the sense of four lines in Henryson in a way to which Gualterus and *Isopet I* offer no equivalent:

> Lat be this hole and cum unto my place.
> I sall you schaw be gude experience
> My Gud Fryday is bettir nor your Pase,
> My dische likking is wirth your haill expens.
>
> (85–88)

The relationship is fairly obvious, but as compared to the French, Henryson's diction is characteristically more vivid and vigorous, and the stylistic level is appreciably lower.

Other notable parallels are also with *Isopet de Lyon*:

> Syne confortit hir with wordis as huny sweit
>
> (154)

> Bel et doucemant la conforte
>
> (XII. 67)

> Thy mangery is myngit all with cair;
> Thy guss is gud, thy ganesall sour as gall
>
> (183–4)

> En boiche trop cusancenouse
> N'est viande bien saverouse.
>
> (XII. 75–76)

These brief examples are perhaps sufficient to establish that Henryson knew and used a French version of Gualterus which must in many ways have resembled, and may have been identical with, *Isopet de Lyon*. The fact is in several ways important. At the present time (and despite the position conceded to La Fontaine in the history of French literature), one inclines to regard the fable as a literary kind naturally and essentially inferior—more suitable for the nursery than the study. The establishment of the tradition in which Henryson, like La Fontaine, wrote, may serve as a

reminder that in the Middle Ages and Renaissance the fable had a
learned Latin background and was of international literary importance. Several factors confirm this reading. The additions to *Isopet I*
were prepared for a French queen, Jeanne de Bourgogne, wife of
Philippe VI who reigned from 1328 to 1350. The author of *Isopet
de Lyon* was a man of some learning, capable of quoting Cicero,
Ovid, Aristotle, and the Bible.[1] As may be illustrated by a few
lines from *Dou Lou et de l'Aignelat*, he was in many ways a master
of narrative and dialogue in the medium of a limpid middle style:

> Grant paour ai, ne seit qu'il face,
> Quar Ysegrins fort le menace.
> «Mavais Aigneax, dit li traïtes,
> A la fontaigne mar venites!
> Vos m'avez corrociez sanz dote,
> L'aigue m'avez troblee tote.»
> L'Aigneax se deffent per raison,
> Dit qu'il n'i pensa traïson;
> Mais sovant trait per sa nature
> L'aigue corrant en soi ordure.
> Avuec ce l'aigue est douce et clere,
> Ne n'est toble ne n'est amere.
> Li Lous crie: «Tu me menaces!»
> — «Ne fès, Sire, salves voz graces,
> Onques nou pensai nois en songe.»
> — «Tai toi, dit li Lous, c'est mançonge.
> Je t'ai cy oï menacier
> De mon domaige porchacier.
> Aussi me fit, et pis essez,
> Tes peres, .VI. mois ai pessez.
> Filz de traitour, or le compere,
> Muer por lo pechié de ton pere!
> Droiz est que tu lo comparoies,
> Quar tu tienz ses mavaises voies.»
>
> (II. 9–32)

---

[1] Bastin, op. cit. II. xxxvii–xxxviii; xviii–xix.

Nor was his stylistic range limited to the middle; it is not an entirely inadequate speech which in *De la Famme qui prist a mari lo Larron* he puts into the mouth of God:

> Li grant juges de veritey
> Respondit pour auctoritey:
> «En nombre, en pois et en mesure
> Fit lo monde qui encor dure
> Ma force; mes senz, ce sez tu,
> Touz jours dure en sa grant vertu.
> Donc puis bien encor mantenir
> Ce que j'ai fait a convenir.
> Dou solat lo cours ordonai:
> Ce tiegne, que je li donai.
> Je sai bien qu'a commun profit
> Li offices de lui soffit.
> Por eschiver si grant domaiges
> Ne voil je que cilz mariaiges
> Per meniere qu'il soit se face.
> Vivez tuit segurs per ma grace.»
>
> (VII. 93–108)

A comparison with the cryptic but meagre Latin of the entire fable in Gualterus may help to establish his imaginative independence and power:

> Femina dum nubit Furi, vicinia gaudet;
> Vir bonus et prudens talia verba movet:
> 'Sol pepigit sponsam; Jovis aurem Terra querelis
> Percutit et causam, cur foret aegra, dedit.
> "Sole necor solo; quid erit, si creverit alter?
> Quid patiar? Quid aget tanta caloris hiems?" '
>
> (VII. 1–6)

In short, the author of *Isopet de Lyon* was as much a creator as a translator, from the example of whose work Henryson learned much of the technique which he used in the *Morall Fabillis*.

APPENDIX III

The *Morall Fabillis* and the Beast-Epic

FIVE of Henryson's *Taillis*, *The Fox and the Wolf*, *The Trial of the Fox*, *The Fox, the Wolf and the Cadger*, *The Fox, the Wolf and the Husbandman*, and *The Cock and the Fox*, are primarily related to the tradition of the beast-epic. Only tenuous links connect them to the main Aesopic tradition. The Aesopic source of *The Fox and the Wolf* is *De Lupo et Mutone*, Fable XLVII in the *Romulus* of Gualterus, to which corresponds Fable XLVII, *Du Loup et du Mouton*, of *Isopet I*, and *Du Loup et du Mouton*, Fable XLI of *Isopet III*.[1] From one or more of these Henryson may have taken at least the idea of the salmon episode. In the French the motives for the wolf's vow are more specifically Christian than in the Latin, and the French may thus have been the more immediate source from which Henryson worked. But he completely transformed even this single episode. The villain of the earlier versions is a wolf, who is forced by illness to vow abstention from meat. One day he meets a lamb, whom he greets as a salmon, 'Saumon, Dieu te gart!' The lamb's protests are over-ridden by the wolf, who devours him. In contrast, Henryson makes his villain a fox, and perhaps for astrological reasons already discussed, he makes the victim a kid. The fox's motives are more elaborate and convincing, and he drowns the kid and turns it into salmon by methods much more vivid than anything in the Latin or French.

Dr. Ian Jamieson has pointed out to me that Odo of Cheriton's *De Asino Nolente Venire ad Parliamentum Leonis*[2] closely parallels *The Trial of the Fox*. The kick given by the mare to the wolf occurs

[1] It is a curious fact that the fable does not appear in the *Isopet de Lyon*. One might also compare Marie de France, *De Lupo et Mutone* (cited by Gregory Smith, *Henryson*, I. xxxv).

[2] C.C.C.C. MS. 441: Hervieux, op. cit. IV.

in Gualterus XLI, *De Equo et Leone*, and in the *Isopets*. In those, as the title indicates, lion is substituted for wolf, horse for mare.

Gualterus and the *Isopets* provide no direct parallels to *The Fox, the Wolf and the Cadger, The Fox, the Wolf and the Husbandman*, or *The Cock and the Fox*. I hope to demonstrate later that Henryson found the source of the second in Caxton's *Aesop*, printed in 1484.

A general source more important than Gualterus and the *Isopets* is Caxton's translation of the Flemish *Die hystorie van Reynaert die Vos, The History of Reynard the Fox*,[1] which appeared in 1481. In *The Fox and the Wolf*, for instance, the fox's confession is at least distantly related to *Reynard*, Chapter XII, 'How the Fox Was Shriven to Grimbert', and Chapter XXVII, 'How the Fox Came Again to the Court and of His Shrift'. In neither of these (nor, so far as I am aware, anywhere else) is the fox's confessor a wolf, but Henryson probably took the idea of a wolf in holy orders from *Reynard* XXVIII, 'How Reynard the Fox Excused Him Before the King'. There Reynard admits that he once 'counselled Isegrim the wolf for to leave his religion at Elmare, and forsake his habit. He complained to me that he lived so straitly as in long fasting and many things reading and singing that he could not endure it.' (p. 126) From the same chapter Henryson took the wolf's name Waitskaith, which in *Reynard* belongs to a Roman cleric, a friend of Martin the Ape. The name seems to appear only in Caxton and Henryson,[2] and is thus decisive for the influence of one upon the other.

Henryson's debt to Caxton is greatest in *The Trial of the Fox*. Apart from Odo of Cheriton's work, the most important identifiable source for the story of the wolf kicked by the mare is *Reynard* XXVII.[3] There the fox tells how he and the wolf were walking

---

[1] D. B. Sands, *The History of Reynard the Fox* (Cambridge, Mass., 1960). This edition is in modern spelling.

[2] Noted by A. R. Diebler, *Henrisone's Fabeldichtungen* (Halle, 1885), p. 46. Diebler was first to notice many of the parallels quoted in this section. His work has in general been much undervalued.

[3] Branch XVI of the *Roman de Renart* 88 (ed. M. Roques, Paris, 1960) contains what is basically the same story, itself derived from the *Romulus*. The fox, however, plays no part, and verbal parallels are missing.

'between Houthulst and Elverding' when they saw a mare with a foal. The wolf was starving and sent Reynard to ask the price of the foal. The mare said it was written on her hinder foot, and when the wolf tried to read it, she kicked and almost killed him. Direct verbal parallels may be drawn with the narrative in Henryson, as for instance (the fox is talking):

'I demanded of her how she would sell it. She said, "It is written on my hinder foot. If you can read and be a clerk, you may come and read it." Tho wist I well where she would be and I said, "Nay, forsooth, I cannot read".' (p. 117)

Henryson's dependence on this is shown by the words which his fox uses:

> 'Laurence, tak you the flirdome and the fon:
> I have a respit heir, and ye will rede.'
> 'I can nocht spell a word, sa God me speid.'   (199–201)

The mare has not mentioned that her respite is written on her hoof, but the fox still denies his ability to read.

A parallelism still more striking occurs when the fox talks to the wolf after the kick:

'Dear eme, is that the truth that you tell me? I have great marvel! I held you for one of the wisest clerks that now live. Now I hear well it is true that I long since have read and heard that the best clerks be not the wisest men.' (p. 118)

Compare the words of the lion[1] when fox and wolf return to court:

> The lyoun said, 'be yone rede cap I ken
> This tale is trew, quha tent unto it takis;
> The grettest clerkis ar nocht the wyssest men.'
>
>   (253–5)

Henryson, however, has not limited himself to a single episode.

---

[1] One should also compare Chaucer, *Reeve's Tale* 4054, 'The gretteste clerkes been noght wisest men, / As whilom to the wolf thus spak the mare.' Chaucer gives the remark to the mare, not the lion.

One of his most attractive inventions is the fox's reference to the wolf's head, bleeding after the kick. He is talking to the lion:

> Than Lourance said 'My lord, spere nocht at me!
> This new maid Doctour of Divinitee
> With his rede cap can tell yow wele yneuch.'
>
> (242–4)

Characteristically, Henryson has himself contributed the doctorate in divinity, but the germ of the concept is to be found in three episodes of *Reynard*. First of these is VIII, 'How Bruin Ate the Honey'. The fox is addressing the wounded bear:

'Dear Eme, tell me ere I go hence into what order will you go that wear this new hood? Were you a monk or an abbot, he that shaved your crown has nipped off your ears. You have lost your top and done off your gloves. I trow verily that you will go sing compline.' (p. 62)

Second is XXXII, 'How the Fox with Subtlety Excused himself ...'. Reynard recalls the words spoken to him by the lion who had wounded the wolf in the head:

'Tho said you, "Reynard, who has taught you to depart so courteously?"'

' "My lord," said I, "that has done this priest that sits here with a bloody crown. He lost his skin with the uncourteous departing of the swine and for his covetous and ravin he has hurt and shame."' (p. 154)

Third may be a phrase from XXXIV, 'A Fair Parable of the Fox and the Wolf'. The fox is describing to the king an adventure which he and the wolf shared:

'See, my lord the king, thus got he his red coif.' (p. 166)

A relationship between the central episode and Caxton's *Reynard* is thus established. The relationship moreover extends to the other parts of the *Taill*. The Parliament of Beasts with the lion as king is modelled on the opening chapters of *Reynard*, and in particular on Chapter 1, 'In the First How the King of All Beasts, The Lion,

Held His Court'. There is one qualification. Henryson to some considerable extent modelled the list of animals who attended the parliament on *Kingis Quair*[1] stanzas 155–7: in particular, there is a self-evident similarity between

> The percyng lynx; the lufare unicorne,
> That voidis venym with his evour horne.
>
> There sawe I dress him newe out of haunt
> The fery tiger, full of felonye;
> The dromydare; the standar oliphant.

and

> The Lynx, the tegir full of tyrrane:
> The oliphant, and eik the dromodare.
>
>   (891–2)

For the rest, however, the details are clearly drawn from Reynard. 'The Nobill Lyoun' derives from Noble, the lion's name in Caxton XIII. In Henryson the Parliament meets on a spring or summer morning:

> The morowing come, and Phebus with his bemys
> Consumit had the mysty cloudis gray.
> The ground was grene, and as the gold it glemys,
> With gresis growand gudelie, grete and gay;
> The spice than spred to spring on every spray;
> The lark, the maviss, and the merle so hee,
> Swetlye can sing, trippand fra tree to tree. (71–77)

Compare the opening of *Reynard*:

'It was about the time of Pentecost or Whitsuntide that the woods commonly be lusty and gladsome and the trees clad with leaves and blossoms and the ground with herbs and flowers sweet smelling and also the fowls and birds sing melodiously in their harmony that the lion, the noble king of all beasts, would in the holy pays of this feast hold an open court at Stade, which he did to know over all his land.' (pp. 45–46)

[1] W. Mackay Mackenzie, *Kingis Quair* (London, 1939).

The type of description is commonplace, but Henryson is closer to
Caxton than to the corresponding passage in, for instance, *Le
Roman de Renart*:[1]

> Ce dist l'estoire es premiers vers
> que ja estoit passez yvers
> et l'aube espine florisoit
> et la rose espannisoit
> et pres fu de l'Acension,
> messires Noble le lyon
> toutes les baisstes fist venir
> en son palais por cort tenir.
>
> (I. 11–18)

In *Reynard* no sooner is the court in session than the animals
begin to complain of the fox. Henryson's fox anticipates just such
an outcome:

> I wait this suddane semblay that I se,
> Havand the poyntis of a parliament,
> Is maid to mar sic misdoaris as me.
>
> (162–4)

In *Reynard*, only the fox fails to attend the court, and messengers
are dispatched to summon him. In Henryson correspondingly only
the 'gray stude meir' is absent, and messengers—the fox and the
wolf—are dispatched to summon her. I have already quoted from
Reynard the fox's description of the wounded Bruin, one of the
messengers sent to his castle; the fate of the bear is very similar to
that of the wolf in Henryson. The hanging of the fox in Henryson
resembles the hanging in *Reynard* XV, with the major difference
that in *Reynard* the fox escapes, but in Henryson he does not.

When the ewe accuses Reynard of killing her lamb, he defends
himself thus:

> My purpois was with him bot to have plaid;
> Caussles he fell, as he had bene affraid;

---

[1] Roques, op. cit. 78 (Paris, 1957), p. 1.

> For drede of dede he duschit our a dike,
> And brak his nek.
>
> $\qquad\qquad\qquad\qquad\qquad\qquad$ (270–3)

The ewe is quick to disprove him:

> His dede be practik may be previt eth:
> Thy gorry gomys and thy bludy snout,
> The woll, the flesche yit stikkis in thy teth.
>
> $\qquad\qquad\qquad\qquad\qquad\qquad$ (274–6)

This may derive from the fox's second confession in *Reynard* XVI:

'Now help Spiritus Domini for I see here no man but I have trespassed unto. Nevertheless, yet was I unto the time that I was weaned from the teat one the best child that could anywhere be found. I went tho and played with the lambs because I heard them gladly bleat. I was so long with them that at last I bit one. There learned I first to lap of the blood. It savored well. Methought it right good. And after I began to taste of the flesh thereof, I was lickerous so that after that I went to the goats into the wood. There heard I the kids bleat and I slew of them twain. I began to wax hardy. After, I slew hens, poultry, and geese wherever I found them. Thus worden my teeth all bloody. After this I waxed so fell and so wroth that whatsomever I found that I might over, I slew all.' (p. 83)

The Fox, the Wolf and the Cadger depends less closely on Caxton. But Diebler and Gavin Bone[1] have indicated the possibility that Henryson used a paragraph from Chapter IV. Grimbert is discussing Reynard with Isegrim:

'Know not you how you misdealed on the plaice which he threw down from the car when you followed after from afar. And you ate the good plaice alone and gave him no more than the grate or bones which you might not eat yourself.' (p. 49)

---

[1] *R.E.S.* x (1934), p. 319. Compare also R. Bauman, 'The Folktale and Oral Tradition in the Fables of Robert Henryson', *Fabula*, VI (1963), pp. 108–24. Mr. Bauman certainly seriously underestimates the value of the literary tradition in which Henryson wrote.

Verbal parallels establish some dependence of *The Fox, the Wolf and the Husbandman* on *Reynard* XXXIII. Compare

> The Tod come hailland up, the Wolf yeid doun;
> Than angerlie the Wolff upon him cryis:
> 'I cummand thus dounwart, quhy thow upwart hyis?'
> 'Schir' (quod the Foxe), 'thus fairis it off Fortoun:
> As ane cummis up, sho quheillis ane uther doun!'
>
> (2415–19)

with

'Then said you, "Aunt, spring into that bucket that hangs there and you shall come anon to me." I did so and I went downward and you came upward. Tho was I all angry. You said, "Thus fares the world. That one goes up and another goes down."'
(p. 160)

As I hope to establish later, the most important feature common to these episodes is the anger of the wolf at the disappearance of the fox.

Henryson, it is thus possible to assume, knew Caxton's *Reynard*, which in turn derives by way of the Flemish from the European beast-epic, best represented by the French *Roman de Renart*. Henryson, however, at least came to have more direct links with the French epic. I have already tried to show that *The Fox, the Wolf and the Cadger* together with *The Fox, the Wolf and the Husbandman,* which must be considered separately, probably belongs to a period later than that of *The Fox and the Wolf* and *The Trial of the Fox.* It should now be clear that it is also more tenuously linked to Caxton's *Reynard.*

The affiliation is in fact directly to the *Roman de Renart.* Caxton's brief reference differs from Henryson in several significant ways. He tells how Isegrim worsted Reynard; Henryson how the fox worsted the wolf. The fish in Caxton are plaice; in Henryson they are herring. In Henryson the fox plays dead; in Caxton he does not. Henryson was quite capable of making these changes for himself, but when the *Roman de Renart* preserves another version of the story, in a language known to Henryson, and in a form closer than Caxton's to that given by Henryson, it is reasonable to assume that Henryson based his work primarily on the *Roman*.

Lines 525–646 of Martin's[1] fourteenth Branch tell how the hungry wolf met the fox who gave him a herring (*heranc*) stolen from a cart by the method also adopted by Henryson's fox:

> Je me chocai enmi la voie
> Et la teste tenoie entort
> Ausi con se je fusse mort.
> Si tost conme li caretier
> Me virent jesir ou senter,
> Si quiderent a escient
> Que je fusse mort vraiement.
> Il me pristrent que n'i ot el,
> Que il dessirroient ma pel.
> Et meintenant me pristrent il,
> Si me jetent el caretil.
>
> (566–76)

The wolf was driven by hunger to try the same trick (there is nothing, it should be noticed, to parallel Henryson's 'nekhering'), but the merchants had learned their lesson, and he was well beaten for his pains:

> Bien est batu por les herens
> Dont il guida avoir sa part.
>
> (628–9)

There is thus no need to assume that Caxton influenced the composition of the *Taill*.

At a first glance, it might appear that *The Fox, the Wolf and the Husbandman* is also to be derived from the *Roman de Renart*, in which may be found some parallel to almost every detail of

---

[1] E. Martin, *Le Roman de Renart*, II (Strasbourg and Paris, 1885), pp. 123–6. Roques's edition does not yet include this Branch. One should also compare Roques, op. cit. 88, pp. 1–15, 'Les poissons dérobés, moniage d'Isengrin et la Pêche au seau'.

Henryson's *Taill*. Thus the wolf misidentifies the reflection of the moon in the well as a great cheese.

> The schadow of the Mone schone in the well.
> 'Schir' (said Lowrence), 'anis ye sall find me leill;
> Now se ye not the Caboik weill your sell,
> Quhyte as ane Neip, and round als as ane seill?'
>
> $(2392–5)$

Branch I of the *Roman*[1] contains a reference to a similar incident. Renart is speaking about Isengrin:

> Gel fis peschier en la fontaine,
> la nuit que la lune fu plaine:
> de l'onbre blanc et de l'image
> cuida por voir ce fust fromage.
>
> $(1075–8)$

I have not been able to find an extended version of this tale in the *Roman*, but Branch II,[2] *C'est la branche come Renart fist Isengrin entrer ou puis*, does contain a differently motivated version of the story of the fox and wolf in the well. The plot is roughly that of the English *The Fox and the Wolf*. The fox descends into the well because he thinks his own reflection is his wife, Hermeline. The wolf in turn thinks that he sees Hersent his wife in Renart's company:

> quida ce fust dame Hersant
> qui herbergiee fust leanz,
> et que Renart fust avec lui.
>
> $(3465–7)$

Isengrin allows himself to be persuaded that Renart and Hersent have died and are in paradise. The buckets are counterbalanced. As Isengrin descends to join them, Renart rises:

> Isengrin l'a araisoné:
> 'Renart, biau frere, ou va tu?'

[1] Roques, op. cit. 78, p. 37.
[2] Roques, op. cit. 79 (Paris, 1951), pp. 1–15.

> Et Renart li a respondu:
> 'N'en faites ja chiere ne frume;
> bien vos en dirai la costume:
> quant li uns va, li autres vient,
> c'est la costume qui avient.
> Ge vois en paradis laisus,
> tu vas ou puis d'enfer lajus.'
>   (3602–10)

This closely resembles the lines of Henryson already quoted.

> Than angerlie the Wolff upon him cryis:
> 'I cummand thus dounwart, quhy thow upwart hyis?'
> 'Schir' (quod the Foxe), 'thus fairis it off Fortoun:
> As ane cummis up, scho quheillis ane uther doun!'
>   (2416–19)

The *Roman*, it should be noticed, makes no reference to the wolf as angry.

The *Roman* has also preserved a variant version of Henryson's introductory episode in *C'est de l'Ors et de Renart et dou vilain Lietart*.[1] In this the bear overhears a ploughman curse his best ox.

> Je voroie que ors et leus
> Vos eüsent ore avoc eus
> Ce peliçon sanz demorance,
> Car pou pris mes vostre puissance.
>   (9325–8)

He attempts to hold the ploughman to the letter of his curse, but with the help of Renart the ploughman outwits him.

Henryson may well have known these episodes and, had no other evidence survived, one might reasonably have concluded that he had himself combined them in one. The total evidence, however, suggests a different conclusion. Henryson's plot in the same combination reappears in at least three other works: the Latin *Disciplina Clericalis* of Petrus Alphonsus, an early twelfth-century Spanish convert from Judaism, who claims that his work is partly

[1] Roques, op. cit. 85 (Paris, 1958), p. 3.

a translation from the Arabic; Conte XXI of the thirteenth-century French *Le Castoiement d'un Père a son Fils*, 'Du Vilein qui dona ses bues au lou'; and Fable 9 from Book VII of Caxton's *Aesop*. The three are closely related.[1] The *Disciplina Clericalis* consists of a number of short tales related by a father for the edification of his son. *Le Castoiement d'un Père a son Fils* is a thirteenth-century Old French translation of the *Disciplina Clericalis*. Book VII of Caxton's *Aesop* is based on the *Disciplina Clericalis* by way of the French translation (1483) by Jules de Machault, of the German Steinhowel's *Äsop* (1480), in which the work of Petrus Alphonsus had been interpolated. Save for the language in which they are written, the three are thus identical even in matters of fine detail. The fact, however, that Henryson made so much use of Caxton elsewhere in the *Fabillis* might incline one to suspect that here too Caxton was his primary source. And in fact there is just evidence enough to suggest that this is a fair reading of the probabilities. Thus, according to the *O.E.D.*, Henryson in this *Taill* is the first in English to use the word 'shadow' in the sense 'reflection of a bright object'. (The sense 'reflection' is found as early as the *Lambeth Homilies*.) It is easy to demonstrate the existence of this sense in French. But of the three possible sources for the *Taill*, only Caxton uses the word 'shadow' as applied to the reflection of the moon. Petrus Alphonsus has 'formam lunae semiplenae in ima putei radiantis ostendit'. (Notice too that the moon here is not full.) *Le Castoiement* follows the Latin.

> Li gopilz le leu apela,
> Et dedenz le puis li monstra
> La forme de la lune plaine.
>   (67–69)

(Here the moon is full.) Caxton is opposed to both.

---

[1] A. Hilka and W. Söderhjelm, *Die Disciplina Clericalis des Petrus Alfonsi* (*Sammlung mittellateinischer Texte I*, Heidelberg, 1911; *Acta Societatis Scientiarum Fennicae*, Helsingfors, 1912, 1922). Both French versions appear in the second and third volumes. Caxton's *Aesop* was edited by J. Jacobs (2 vols., London, 1889).

'They came to a welle / vpon the whiche the Foxe lepte / and shewed to the wulf the shadowe of the mone / which reluced in the well . . .' (p. 277)

One other feature, common to Caxton and Henryson, but unparalleled in the other two versions, is the exchange between fox and wolf as one descends and the other rises. In Caxton it runs thus:

'and whan the wulf sawe the Foxe comynge vpward / he sayd to hym / My godsep ye goo hens / thow sayst trewe sayd the Fox / For thus hit is of the world / For when one cometh doune / the other goth vpward.' (p. 278)

I have already indicated the similarities between the corresponding passage in Henryson, Caxton's *Reynard* and the *Roman de Renart*. One might deduce that when Caxton came to this episode of his *Aesop* he recollected the similar passage in his *Reynard* and transferred the remark from one to the other. Henryson also seems to have noted the similarity. As I have indicated, the wolf's anger in Henryson, unparalleled as it is in any of the more direct sources, is found in Caxton's *Reynard*.

Although *The Taill of Schir Chantecleir and the Foxe* has much in common with the four *Taillis* just discussed, nothing like it appears in the *Romulus* of Gualterus, in the *Isopets* or in the *Reynard* of Caxton. A somewhat different version is preserved in the *Roman de Renart*. Harvey Wood seems to believe that Henryson made an adaptation from popular tradition; at least, in his Commentary[1] he quotes James I's line from the *Kingis Quair*,

> The wyly fox the wedowis inemye
>
>   (156)

as evidence that by the fifteenth century the central theme of the fable had passed into proverbial use. But that is almost to dodge the issue. The *Kingis Quair* is saturated with Chaucerian reminiscences, and as Mackay Mackenzie suggested,[2] the line may well be a direct

[1] Op. cit., p. 229.   [2] Mackay Mackenzie, op. cit., p. 120.

reference to the *Nun's Priest's Tale* of Chaucer. This is the more likely because versions of the tale, other than those of Chaucer and Henryson, make Chantecleir belong, not to a widow, but a rich farmer, as for instance in the *Roman de Renart*:[1]

> et messires Coutenz des Noes,
> uns vilains qui mout iert garniz,
> manoit mout pres dou plaissaïz.
> (4072–4)

The differences between the *Nun's Priest's Tale* and the *Taill of Schir Chantecleir* are numerous—most notably, Henryson's version has nothing like the dream which in Chaucer Chauntecleir and Pertelote discuss at such learned length, while Chaucer has nothing like the 'disputatioun' of Pertok, Sprutok, and Toppok. Henryson indeed seems to have based the names of Chantecleir's wives on the *Tale of Colkelbie Sow*,[2] III. 99–120. Nevertheless, I believe that Henryson's *Taill*, in its essential shape, is an adaptation of Chaucer's. Henryson has transformed it, partly, it may be, to make it conform to the pattern of *The Fox and the Wolf*, partly also as a consequence of the imaginative and intellectual experience of the composition of *Orpheus and Eurydice*, to which the *Taill* forms a comic equivalent.

[1] Roques, op. cit. 79, pp. 26 ff.   [2] Tod Ritchie, op. cit. IV. 279 ff.

INDEX

PRINTED IN GREAT BRITAIN
AT THE UNIVERSITY PRESS, OXFORD
BY VIVIAN RIDLER
PRINTER TO THE UNIVERSITY